MW01001954

SUPER SUNDAY SCHOOLS
IN THE
BLACK
COMMUNITY

Sid Smith

BROADMAN PRESS
Nashville, Tennessee

© Copyright 1986 ● Broadman Press
All rights reserved
4262-52
ISBN: 0-8054-6252-X
Dewey Decimal Classification: 268
Subject Headings: SUNDAY SCHOOLS - BLACKS // BLACK CHURCHES
Library of Congress Catalog Number: 86-926
Printed in the United States of America
All Scripture references are from the King James
Version of the Holy Bible.

Library of Congress Cataloging-in-Publication Data

Smith, Sid.
  10 super Sunday Schools in the Black community.

  1. Afro-American Sunday Schools.   2. Afro-American
Baptists.   I. Title.   II. Title: 10 super Sunday Schools
in the Black community.
BV1523.A37S65   1986   268'.861'08996073   86-926
ISBN 0-8054-6252-X

Contents

Foreword

Sid Smith has given us a book that is one of a kind. His message is: "Black Sunday Schools can grow; black churches can reach and teach more people through effective use of the Sunday School than they have ever reached before." In fact, some black churches are doing it right now. That's what this book is all about. It is the exciting and encouraging story of ten black churches that are reaching vast numbers of people, and they are using the Sunday School to do it!

Sid Smith clearly and effectively shows the open door of opportunity that black churches have through using the Sunday School to its fullest advantage. I strongly urge the widest distribution and use of this book to all who are seeking to reach the black community of this nation.

Harry Piland, Director, Sunday School Department, Baptist Sunday School Board

Preface

Dr. Smith has for nearly twenty years served Southern Baptists with the Home Mission Board, the Sunday School Board, and as pastor and minister of religious education. He knows Southern Baptists in general, and black Southern Baptists in particular, as well or better than any person today. He knows strong Sunday Schools will grow strong churches.

"Ten Super Sunday Schools" is the exciting story of great churches whose leadership has found the Sunday School a key to their ministry. Dr. Smith has an evangelistic heart with a mind for religious education, who feels the latter serves the former wonderfully and effectively.

Bob Boyd, Supervisor, Black Church Development Section, BSSB

Introduction

The church is the most significant institution in America's black community. It plays an Herculean role in the development of the people. This giant of progress is involved. Without the ministry of the church, chains of bondage, veils of ignorance, and burdens of restriction would still be upon America's ebony citizens.

Despite being a drum major for justice, it has often led a marching band with some instruments omitted. In certain areas the church has blown an uncertain sound. Honest analysis compels the conclusion that while the church in the black community has been strong, it has also been far from perfect. Like churches from every ethnic/racial community, black congregations have both strengths and weaknesses.

A major problem area for most black churches is the crisis in religious education. In a day when there is a flood of religious education resources, many black churches are thirsty for programs which will equip them to master the complexities of life. In today's high-tech society many churches still operate religious education programs with a horse-and-buggy mentality. In our space-age world, many churches operate with stone-age methodology.

Nowhere is the crisis of religious education more acute than in the Sunday School. During the past one hundred years the emphasis on black Sunday School work has regressed from high priority to minimal attention. Churches that majored on the Sunday School a century ago now minor on it. The point seems to have been forgotten that a church is really no stronger than its religious education program. The heart of the religious education program is the Sunday School ministry. To neglect the Sunday School program means to handicap the religious education of the church.

Yes, there is a crisis in black Sunday School work. This phenomenon is manifested in various ways. A critical analysis of the state of Black Sunday School work reveals several debilitating characteristics reflecting this crisis.

First, there appears to be a boycott of Sunday School attendance by most church members. While "boycott" may be too strong to describe adequately the phenomenon, the fact remains that most blacks do not attend Sunday School. Estimated black Sunday School attendance is projected at probably no more than 15 percent in most churches. It is as though most blacks have concluded that they do not need Sunday School!

A second manifestation of this crisis is reflected in the lack of attention given to the subject by curriculum developers. To date, books on the subject are almost nonexistent, and courses on black Sunday School growth are extremely rare. There is also a shortage of training.

A third manifestation is the lack of attention to Sunday School given by many black pastors. Pastors often have little grasp of the significance of Sunday School growth. Sunday School is often among the lowest priorities under his leadership. In many cases, he himself may not even attend Sunday School. Unwittingly, many pastors generate a "negative pastoral leadership syndrome" by unintentionally emitting signals through their body language which convey the message that Sunday School is not important.

The existence of this crisis has generated tremendous

needs. Neglect of this vital area leads to mountainous problems for the church. A generation without systematic Bible study results in a generation of biblical illiterates; stunted spiritual growth results from biblical malnutrition. Churches function at only a small percent of their potential when Sunday School is neglected. Members are minimally equipped for their ministry without the effective Sunday School experience. Members who attend churches with little or no qualitative Sunday School involvement are cheated of their right to maximum service from their church. Sunday School neglect leads to the assumption that education is not inextricably related to a meaningful, growing, qualitative Christian experience. When churches neglect the Sunday School, the people are hurt.

However, it is encouraging that the story does not end on that sour note. We live in a day that offers hope for black Sunday School involvement. While thousands of churches suffer from the "mini-Sunday School," others are blooming examples of reaching the community through the Sunday School. An ever-growing number of churches in the black community have discovered how to build dynamic, growing, quality Sunday Schools! They are making tremendous progress flying against the headwinds of cultural apathy and neglect. They provide models which prove it is possible to reach the black community through the Sunday School.

The purpose of this book is to share how ten churches in the black community have developed dynamic, super Sunday Schools. The focus will be primarily on numerical growth. Of course, other aspects of growth need to be treated, but that task remains for another inquiry. It is hoped that the reports on how these churches grow exceptional Sunday Schools will inform and inspire others to emulate their example.

In a day when neglect of Sunday School dominates, this

book recognizes that there are alternatives to neglect. There are heroic examples of Sunday School success! It is not necessary for pastors and leaders burdened with a desire for growth to languish in the frustration of the unknown. The expertise is now available on how to grow super Sunday Schools in the black community. This work is an attempt to analyze and share that expertise. Hopefully, many churches will catch the vision and become masters of Sunday School growth.

It is the writer's position that understanding principles of black Sunday School growth presents a tremendous opportunity for the advancement of church life in the black community. What if the situation of the "mini-Sunday School" could be transformed into the "maxi-Sunday School?" More people could be won to Christ; church membership would increase dramatically; Bible knowledge would tremendously increase; church budgets could multiply. More Christian social ministries could emerge; missions programs would be strengthened; social action ministries could have greater support; the quality of the comprehensive Christian experience would greatly improve. What an opportunity!

This inquiry is governed by certain limitations. It is restricted in several areas. Five areas of restriction include the following:

First, it is limited to black Baptists with one exception. This is not to minimize the importance of other denominations with black presence. It is merely a pragmatic restriction due to the researcher's limitation of time and resources.

Second, it is limited by focusing primarily on numerical growth. The thrust of the inquiry is on the subject of reaching people through the Sunday School. It focuses on successful growth strategies in the black community.

Third, it deals only with the definition of the classical Sunday School. That is, only Sunday Schools in the traditional sense were included. The primary characteristic in this determination was a church having a formal Sunday School organization.

Fourth, it is limited by statistical unreliability in some cases. Many churches have incomplete record systems. Therefore, the pastor's estimate had to be accepted as definitive.

Fifth, the information is dated. It is current only through June 1985. Consequently, much of the statistical data probably will have changed. However, the thrust of the story will be a fair representation of the churches' history of Sunday School growth.

It is not an attempt to classify an elite group of churches as champions of Sunday School growth. It is merely an attempt to tell the story of ten churches in the black community with effective, growth-oriented Sunday Schools and how they reach people.

The basic approach to information gathering for this inquiry was complex. Every pastor and Sunday School director were interviewed. Additionally, a tape recording was made of the interviews. A questionnaire was used to guide the discussion, and a visit was made to each church. Most of the information was based on numerous interviews with the pastors.

The results of these experiences are reported in this work. A chapter is devoted to a report on the Sunday School of each of the ten churches.

Greatest appreciation is expressed to the ten churches and pastors which were so gracious in providing the information on which this study is based. Intense gratitude is due the Black Church Development unit of the Baptist Sunday School Board which made this work possible.

1

The Glendale Baptist Church Miami, Florida
Rev. Joseph C. Coats, Pastor

On First Glance

The hustle and bustle of the Sunday morning experience electrified the atmosphere at the Glendale Baptist Church. People could be seen going and coming from every direction with eager anticipation to reach the house of the Lord. In a day when many churches have almost given up on Sunday School, there is a new realization that it is possible to reach many through the Sunday School.

The warm Florida sun is consistent with the heat of the excitement radiating from this congregation. An event is happening here. The humdrum experience of tedium is nowhere found. At 9:30 on Sunday morning, the Glendale Baptist Church is a church on the move. It is busily engaged in reaching almost 2,000 people through the Sunday School program! So effective is its Sunday School program that if one does not attend Sunday School, it is difficult to find a seat in the eleven o'clock service. When it comes to the Sunday School, this church is on fire!

The huge, well-appointed, white stucco buildings are a testimony to the fact that people can indeed be reached through the Sunday School today. For a church approximately twenty years old, the Glendale Baptist Church has experienced phenomenal growth. Church leaders ascribe this growth largely to the effectiveness of the Sunday School program, which has top priority. Evidence of this priority is found in the recent addition of a new educational building providing approximately one hundred classrooms for Sunday School. The grounds of the church reflect a pride in accomplishment and achievement for the Lord. The well-landscaped scenery provides a monument that says, "We have a big God, and we are proud of the fact." The emphasis on its building space reflects the conviction of the church that it ought to be primarily a religious education institution equipping people to live victoriously in the everyday world.

At 8:30 AM on Sunday, a band of Sunday School workers joins hands for prayer in preparation for Sunday School. The pastor, Rev. Joseph C. Coats, stands in the middle of his army of workers and prayerfully invites the power of the Lord to be upon His people that day. An aura of reverence permeates the gathering as if the presence of the Lord has suddenly been manifested, and everyone knows that "Surely the Lord is in this place." A climate of consecration is immediately apparent to the onlooker as the experience of preparation is culminated through this prayer period one hour before Sunday School.

The most prominent person among the group of pray-ers is the pastor. He is a heavyset man of average height with broad shoulders and the appearance of a spiritual general. His stance is one of leading troops into battle, not sending them. Pastor Coats is a man of tremendous ability and insight in church administration. His intelligence in the area of Sunday School growth is among the best in the country. He has the vision to put together the best in Sunday School theory and practical application. He is a leader who has mastered practical theology. Obviously a man who loves the Lord, he has been the key leader in building this "mega

Sunday School" which has been called by some: "The largest Sunday School in the black community in America."

The Glendale Baptist Church does have the distinction of being one of the most effective churches in the area of Sunday School work. How does the church do it? How does it buck the trend of apathy toward Sunday School in the black community and succeed in enlisting the participation of almost 2,000 people? What set of dynamics are operative in this situation? What lessons will the church have for society as it relates to the question of church growth in the inner city?

The Ekklesia

A visitor once commented, "I don't think I could qualify for membership at the Glendale Baptist Church." As he visited the morning service, the dedication of the people was so immense that he immediately developed an inferiority complex about the quality of his own Christianity. When one goes to the Glendale Baptist Church, one fact is quite obvious: This is a church on mission for the Lord! It appears to be a standard church. Quality is written over all it does. If there ever were a church serious about its commitment to Christ, this is it. On a rating scale of one to ten, it would easily rank close to the top. One receives the impression that it could easily make any objective list of "the great churches in America" today. It appears to have the motto that says: "If the Lord commands us to do it, we will try to do it!"

The history of the Glendale Baptist Church goes back to 1963. The church was organized by the Reverend J. A. Harrington with a handful of members in his home. After two years of existence and the leaving of Rev. Harrington, the church called the Rev. Joseph Coats to be its second pastor.

The Rev. Coats felt called to be an evangelist; so his priority was winning people to the Lord through faith in Jesus Christ. He had a burning zeal to see people come to know Jesus as Lord and Savior.

Under the leadership of Pastor Coats, the church joined the Miami Baptist Association, affiliated with Southern Baptist Convention, and proceeded to have a steady growth in membership down through the years. Pastor Coats applied his fervent evangelistic spirit to the challenge of reaching more people for the Lord. He also utilized the proven, effective methodology of the Southern Baptist Sunday School program in growing his church. Utilizing the basics of Sunday School growth, within the context of cultural adaptation to meet the needs of his flock, he discovered a powerful combination for growing a "megachurch" in a contemporary society. As the church grew it assumed a certain character of its own as it was able to reach more people.

An observer of the Glendale Baptist Church will discover several characteristics of its membership. Perhaps these dynamics enable it to be the fast-growing church it is today. Perhaps these qualities serve as the basis for a magnetism that attracts the multitudes from the Greater Miami area.

What is Glendale Baptist Church like?

First, it is theologically conservative. The Bible is taken quite seriously to be the inspired Word of God, and there is not a discussion of liberal tendencies at all. The pastor is the resident theologian, and he comes from a conservative theological background. The debate raging within many circles of the church today as it relates to "the liberals versus the conservatives" is not found in this church. There is a reverence for the Word of God and an acceptance of it as being regulatory for the behavior of the church.

Second, it is readily apparent that the church is a quality church.
When a person attends, he/she becomes immediately aware
that this is a church striving to do things right. A wide
variety of programs exists to serve the needs of a wide
variety of members. Creative programming occurs within its
walls, and outside of its walls, as it takes seriously the commandment to carry the gospel to all people. The church
attempts to emulate New Testament methodology in terms
of acting out its role in contemporary society. It prides itself
in being a New Testament church. The pastor is often heard
to remark, "We try to do it like Jesus did it."

*Third, in the Glendale Baptist Church, Sunday School is given the
highest priority.* It is not a neglected stepchild program, not
something tolerated because of tradition. It is not merely a
functionary assignment based on history; it is not a program
people take lightly. No, it is a program deemed to be among
the highest emphases in the church. Every member of the
church is expected to become actively involved in the Sunday School. For example, this is shown in the practice of
assigning new members to a Sunday School class as soon as
they join the church. The idea at the Glendale Baptist
Church is: Sunday School is not optional for its membership.
It is recommended as being normal for regular church involvement.

Fourth, there is an emphasis on the practical application of the gospel.
Programs are profound but simple at this church. The
philosophy of the church is that Christianity ought to be a
way of life, and the church has the responsibility of equipping people to live out their Christian life-styles in ministry.
The leadership makes sure that everyone understands exactly what is offered and how every member may fit into the
program. There is no desire to complicate the communica-

tion of the gospel to people, lest there be fuzziness in their understanding as to the requirements for Christian living. Pastor Coats feels it is the responsibility of the church to train the members, so they may understand how to be Christlike.

Fifth, outreach is a major emphasis of this church. The members are not satisfied to be content with merely holding the members they already have. They have a burning desire to go out and reach more people. Outreach programs permeate many of the emphases at the church. There is a desire to enlarge their fellowship and bring in people who previously had not known about the Lord. The church characterizes itself as "a caring, sharing, and giving church." The church views itself as an expanding fellowship of believers with the responsibility to reach new people for Jesus Christ.

Sixth, the Glendale Baptist Church believes in equipping people with tools for performing the work of the ministry. Training is a tremendous emphasis in this church. When the pastor is asked what he does in order to grow a large church, he inevitably responds, "Love the people and train them." This seems to be the motto of Glendale. Although it is famous for having a mega Sunday School, it is also well-known for effective reaching people for training through its Church Training program. On a given Sunday, there will be approximately 500 persons in attendance at Church Training.

Seventh, this church strives for unity in the membership. It does not insist on uniformity—it insists on unity. The church does not expect everyone to think alike. It does expect for everybody, however, to be on the same team and to be committed to the same goals. The church is led by a gifted administrator who has been successful in promoting and maintaining a spirit of unity in the church. Pastor Coats is a master practitioner of church administration, and he has mastered the art of leading the church to go in the same direction.

Eighth, the Glendale Baptist Church is concerned about the holistic needs of persons. It has not divided up the function of the church into evangelism versus social concerns. It embraces the philosophy that the church ought to be concerned about the totality of human existence. The church is not indifferent and apathetic to human needs amid a sea of human suffering. In its program are at least twenty-five different Christian social ministries in operation at a given time. There are programs in the areas of: chemical abuse, senior citizen's ministry, jail ministry, literacy training, migrant ministry, ministry to street people, ministry to youth, a tutorial program involving at least twenty school teachers, a Girl Scout program, a full-time preschool academy during the week, a community evangelistic crusade, and a radio ministry. This church attempts to be relevant to the total needs of persons in the community. When a person looks at the Glendale church, he/she immediately becomes aware that it views itself as a beacon light of hope to hurting humanity. In its community, it shines as a glowing example of what God can do through redeemed human beings.

When a person visits Glendale, he becomes aware of the fact that "Surely the Lord is in this place." One also becomes aware that here is a church which believes, in the words of its pastor: "a church should be like a thermostat and not a thermometer. A thermometer is changed by its environment, but a thermostat changes its environment."

Joshua

Glendale has experienced phenomenal growth under the
pastoral leadership of Pastor Coats. From whence cometh
this Joshua?

Coats is a native of Alamo, Georgia. He graduated from
high school in Miami, Florida, and spent one year in college
before enrolling in the Southern Bible College in Kansas
City, Missouri, where he earned a bachelor of theology degree. He has studied in the Southern Baptist Seminary Extension Program for more than seven years, earning a total
of in excess of one hundred hours credit in Bible study.
Pastor Coats is largely a self-educated pastor who has
earned a reputation as being "a genius of church growth."
He married the former Katherine Williams of Holly Hill,
South Carolina, and together they are the parents of eight
children. Pastor Coats is a dedicated husband and father
who cherishes the time he spends with his family. He does
not allow the church to dominate his schedule but makes
sure that a part of his responsibility is tending to the needs
of his family by spending time with them.

Coats is a man who is clearly well respected by his peers.
There is a sense of reverence on the lips of many who know
him and who have seen his ministry in action. He carries
himself as a minister of the gospel in such a manner as to
earn the admiration of those with whom he closely associ-
ates. In describing him, one of the deacons quietly confided,
"Our pastor is a man of God." Based on his long history of
outstanding consistency and the testimony of his contempo-
raries, to know him is to respect him.

Glendale's pastor is tremendously dedicated to the Lord.
His dedication is single-minded. He seems to live for no
other purpose than to magnify his Lord. If there is a major
league for dedicated Christians, Pastor Coats would be one

of the stars. He is a man characterized by giving all to his ministry for the Lord. In recent years he has been warned to slow down because of the magnitude of the work. However, his reply has been, "I would rather burn out than rust out for my God." He has no greater joy than to be actively involved in serving the Lord.

Pastor Coats, affectionately known as Brother Joe among many of his friends, is also a man of tremendous faith. He practices a personal relationship with God and believes that the Lord leads him personally. He believes the Lord has the ability to do whatever He wants to do. He believes that if we make ourselves available and attempt what the Lord would lead us to do, then the Lord will be able to do mighty things through us. As a result of this philosophy he has been able to build one of the largest Sunday Schools in America, grow a church membership to almost 3,000 persons, start various ministries to meet human needs, and plant a number of missions that have becoming growing and thriving churches on their own.

Several years ago when the church had outgrown its Sunday School space, Pastor Coats led the membership to build a massive new educational building which would provide expanded room for reaching people, and they accepted the challenge to pay for it as they built it! It required considerable faith to do that, but he had an ample amount.

When a person accompanies the pastor of Glendale during the week, he will quickly discover that this minister is always on call for the Lord. Wherever he goes, he has the ministry of the church on his heart and mind. As he travels in elevators he figures out ways to witness. In restaurants he frequently asks the waitresses if they know Jesus. As he walks down the street he braves opposition to inquire about the spiritual welfare of the people he encounters. It seems as though his whole life is geared to leading people into a

saving knowledge of Jesus Christ. To be around him is to be
infected by the enthusiasm of his desire to witness for his
Lord. A weaker Christian will be convicted by the zeal with
which Pastor Coats tries to win people to Christ. If he were
a doctor, he would be considered perpetually on call.

Brother Joe is a pastor with a recognizably brilliant mind.
He has deep analytical ability and has a profound reservoir
of common sense. He has a keen understanding of human
nature and, like Jesus, he knows what is in humankind.
Brother Joe's knowledge of the Word of God is superior.
When involved in conferences with other pastors, he clearly
shines as a person who has a superior intellect. In terms of
creatively building a church program, he is able to grasp the
dynamics and develop practical, operative strategies which
work in the context of his situation.

Sunday morning worship at the Glendale Baptist Church
is an exciting experience. Led by the dynamic, energetic
pastor, the worship service leads one into the realization that
one is in the presence of God. Brother Joe's preaching style
is characterized by a powerful delivery and profound but
simple illustrations. Expository preaching is his forté, and he
cherishes the art of being able to interpret the Word of God
for his congregation. His sermons are simple, interesting,
humorous, and yet profound.

At the worship service, the sermon is the magnificent
event manifesting the visitation of the Word of the Lord to
the congregation through the pastor. His mighty pulpit ability elicits many "amens" from the worshipers. His spiritual
insight illuminates obscure passages of Scripture for the ears
of the listeners. His competence presents this conclusion: If
it can be understood, Brother Joe can make you understand
it. While he is not known as a "whooper," he does have the
oratorical style of the traditional black preacher. This gifted

watchman can bring his congregation closer to heaven through the skill of his gifted oratory.

Pastor Coats is an able equipper of people. When a person goes to Glendale, he expects to be equipped for the task of the gospel. A wide variety of classes is offered on many subjects applicable to the seeking Christian. The latest methodology is in use at the church. The pastor stays alert to new trends in the area of religious education and employs them in the life and ministry of his church. One of the effects of the ministry of Glendale is that people get "turned on" to many possibilities of growth as the result of participation.

In the arena of denominationalism, the pastor is recognized as a leader. He is the pastor of the first black Southern Baptist church in the Florida Baptist Convention. His leadership ability within the Convention has been recognized through his selection to many important positions therein. For example, he has served as moderator, vice-moderator, and president of the Pastors' Conference for the Miami Baptist Association. For the Florida Baptist Convention, he has served as a member of the State Mission Board, the Children's Home Board, and the Board of Trustees for the Baptist Hospital. He is also widely recognized and used as a speaker and conference leader across the Southern Baptist Convention. He has been a speaker and seminar leader at the national conference centers at Glorieta, New Mexico, and Ridgecrest, North Carolina.

In short, Pastor Coats is progressive, bold, and respected. He loves people and is committed to doing his dead-level best to make sure they receive equipping for the work of the church.

Teaching Them All Things

What kind of church attracts almost 2,000 people to its Sunday School program in a day when the mini-Sunday School is the norm? What dynamics are at work in Glendale yielding such a tremendous response to the religious education program offered? How do they do it? How do they challenge the mistaken notion that it is almost impossible to reach the black community through the Sunday School?

Part of the answers to these questions are found in the philosophy of the pastor as it relates to the purpose of the church. In the mind of Pastor Coats, "God's purpose for the church is to cross all barriers of age, social status, nationality, race, and interests, for the purpose of creating one body in Christ, a fellowship of equally condemned and forgiven sinners." He believes there are five spiritual purposes of the church:

1. Worship
2. Witness
3. Education
4. Ministry
5. Application

The Glendale Baptist Church is in the process of being on mission to implement these five spiritual purposes. Pastor Coats's conviction is that "the best-organized church today is one where the pastor is equipping the saints for the task of missions, stewardship, and discipleship." He continues, "If a pastor is to be spiritually successful, he must train his people and share these tasks with them."

According to Pastor Coats, the New Testament spells out how we should accomplish our task of training and teaching in the church. He therefore tries to emulate the New Testament approach as it relates to building his model of religious education. Therefore, much emphasis is placed on the doctrine of the Bible, the doctrine of God, the doctrine of man, and the doctrine of salvation. Heavy emphasis is placed on the spirit of 2 Timothy 2:15, which says, "Study to shew thyself approved unto God, a workman that needeth not to be ashamed, rightly dividing the word of truth."

What does a Sunday School approaching an enrollment of 2,000 look like? What are some of the characteristics of it?

The Sunday School at Glendale has for its theme: "Endeavoring to keep the unity of the spirit in the bond of peace." The pastor strongly believes that one concept must always be maintained in each person's mind: "As the Sunday School goes, so goes the church." Therefore, considerable attention is given to developing a strong Sunday School in order to have a powerful, viable church.

What about the structure of the Sunday School? The Glendale Sunday School has the following breakdown: the Preschool Division, the Children's Division, the Youth Division, and the Adult Division. Each division has several categories of groupings. The Preschool Division is divided into three groups. Group 1: from birth through one year of age; Group 2: from two to three years of age; Group 3, from four to five years of age. The Children's Division also has three groupings. The first grouping is the six- and seven-year-olds. The second grouping is from eight to nine years of age. The third grouping is from ten to eleven years of age.

In the Youth Division, the Sunday School is divided into two groupings. The first is twelve through fourteen years of age, referred to as Younger Youth. The second is fifteen through seventeen years of age, referred to as Older Youth.

The Adult Division is divided into five different groupings. There are (1) the single females in groups of ages from eighteen through twenty-one, twenty-two through twenty-five, and twenty-six through twenty-nine. A second group of adults is the single males from ages eighteen through twenty-nine. The third group is the married females in age groups from eighteen through twenty-four; twenty-five through twenty-nine; thirty through thirty-nine; forty through forty-five; forty-six through fifty; fifty-one through fifty-nine; and sixty and up.

The fourth group of adults is the married males, divided into ages eighteen through twenty-nine; thirty through thirty-nine; forty through forty-nine; and fifty and up. The fifth group is the single-again group. This structural pattern is one adopted from the book *Working in Sunday School* by A. V. Washburn and Donald F. Trotter. It is a classical Southern Baptist Sunday School approach to class structure.

In addition to a comprehensive structure for Sunday School involvement, Glendale has made a commitment to growing through the Sunday School. This church has been willing to pay the price in order to prove that people can be reached through the Sunday School. Good Sunday School work does not happen by accident in this church. It happens by intentionality and planning.

The pastor is the leading role model of commitment to the Sunday School. He believes in it; he is involved in it; he is the leader of the program; he has led his church to make it a priority in the life of the church.

A major characteristic of the Glendale Sunday School is its well-trained teachers. According to the pastor: "A Sunday School is no better than the plans it makes. Individual and group planning are conducted on a weekly basis. Ideas are shared by each teacher so that the lessons taught on Sunday morning are of one accord." This church embraces the wisdom of the statement by John T. Sisemore: "Poor teaching will empty a classroom faster than a good outreach program will fill it." Teacher training is not optional at Glendale. It is mandatory. Training for Sunday School workers is conducted during the Church Training hour. The latest in training resources is made available to the teaching staff of the church. Many books on Sunday School work are taught, and workers are expected to earn certificates of proficiency in their area of work.

In the program of this Sunday School, the teachers are expected to meet high standards. Each teacher is expected to be a born-again Christian, have a strong love for people, and have a desire to reach the lost for Jesus Christ. A strong prayer life is also a prerequisite. In this church, not just anybody can teach Sunday School. The persons must be willing to pay the price to be spiritually effective.

A distinguishing mark of the Glendale Sunday School is its distinctive adult emphasis. Many adults are involved in the Sunday School program. This church is not one that believes Sunday School is for children only. It believes Sunday School is for the entire family. When asked how they succeed in attracting so many adults to Sunday School, one Sunday School worker replied, "We make it so interesting when they come that they are eager to come back."

There is an evangelistic emphasis in the Sunday School program at Glendale. Teachers and workers are expected to be soul-winners who are able to share their faith through the Sunday School. A Sunday School worker's labor is not done until there has been the extending of the opportunity for someone to invite Jesus Christ to be the Lord of his or her life. Teachers make it their business to know the spiritual status of the people with whom they come in contact through the Sunday School. Many baptisms result from the conscientious efforts of Sunday School workers to introduce people to Jesus Christ.

Outreach is not done by accident at this church. There is

a distinct plan for reaching new people through the church for the Lord. A well-organized outreach ministry is in place. Workers are trained in the various aspects of reaching out to new persons. A well-documented prospect file is kept and updated periodically so that it will be current. New persons who are potential members of the church and the Sunday School are contacted through the Sunday School Outreach Program and invited to become involved. This Sunday School program does not "shoot at everybody" in general. It targets specific persons who are known to be in its prospect file. The goal of the outreach director is to have a number of persons in the outreach file equivalent to the enrollment of the Sunday School.

The visitor to Glendale will be immediately impressed with the size of the educational facilities. Approximately one hundred Sunday School classrooms are available to house the multitudes which come to Sunday School. This church believes in providing adequate space for the training of persons. It sees and understands the relationship between the provision of sufficient space and the quality of teaching. Even before building its new education building, the church managed to provide teaching spaces in the sanctuary, in the fellowship hall, on the sidewalk, on the lawn, in the buses, and wherever people could be taught the Word of God. They have an appreciation for the relationship between the provision of space and qualitative teaching experiences.

Visitation is an important part of outreach at Glendale. Visitation is conducted through the Sunday School via a systematic visitation program conducted each week. Outreach directors are involved and provide leadership in visiting members, prospects, and persons in need. The practice of this church is: "We must go where the people are with the gospel." So they have a visitation program that allows them to extend far into the community with the message.

One of the characteristics of the Sunday School program Glendale is the willingness to start new classes. There is the philosophy that new classes tend to grow faster than old ones. The people are not reluctant to step out and start a new class as a means of reaching more people. Because of this philosophy, old classes are not threatened by the starting of new classes. Not only do they start new classes, but they also start new Sunday Schools. This church has started a number of mission Sunday Schools in new churches that have gone on to develop into strong congregations on their own.

When asked about the key ingredient for success in reaching so many persons, Pastor Coats is quick to ascribe that success to the effectiveness of the prayer lives of the persons involved. He believes that every action in the church ought to be thoroughly bathed in prayer. Praying to the Lord about the matter will give the Sunday School movement a power it would otherwise not have. One trait about this pastor and Sunday School staff is their insistance upon and dependence upon prayer as an ingredient in the Sunday School.

The testimony of Pastor Coats is this: "Our steady growth has been the result of our Sunday School emphasis—the Southern Baptist Sunday School program. Using Southern Baptist literature has provided us the opportunity to have the finest resources available. These materials work in our situation, and we thank God for them."

The above are ingredients in the success of the Sunday School at the Glendale Baptist Church. When Pastor Coats is asked about his formula for success, he replies, "Work hard. Love the people. Depend on the Holy Spirit. And use the resources of the denomination. They will help your church grow."

2

Emmanuel Baptist Church
San Jose, California
Dr. Willie Gaines, Pastor

Upon Arrival . . .

The hazy California sun dominates the sky. The energy of the hustle and bustle of San Jose, California, permeates the neighborhood. The foot of a mini-mountain range creates a formidable wall that defines an edge of the community. The traffic on North White Road creates a snake of activity on this balmy Sunday morning.

This neighborhood of homes valued in excess of $100,000 sits quietly in reverence. At 467 North White Road, a beautiful complex of Spanish architecture covers the block. This is the Emmanuel Baptist Church in San Jose, California.

The church is located in a community made up of a rainbow of Californians. An estimated 10,000 people live within a two and one-half-mile radius of this church. The ethnic composition of this mosaic is said to be approximately 50 percent Anglo, 40 percent Hispanic, 5 percent Black, and 5 percent others.

The Emmanuel Baptist Church is an exceptional church—for three paramount reasons. First, its pastor, Dr. Willie T. Gaines, is the president of the Southern Baptist General Convention of California. He is the fifth black person to be elected to the top position in a predominantly white Southern Baptist state convention. Second, this church has experienced phenomenal growth as a predominantly black congregation in a predominantly non-black community. Third, in a day when it is viewed as almost impossible to induce large numbers of persons from the black community to attend Sunday School, the Emmanuel Baptist Church Sunday School has been able to attract 1,100 plus in enrollment and has a goal of enrolling 2,000 by the end of 1986!

Upon arrival at the Emmanuel Baptist Church, the visitor is immediately impressed with the fact that this is no ordinary church. It is one of the outstanding churches of our day.

What accounts for that? How does it build a dynamic congregation in a black minority community? How does it attract more than a thousand persons to its Sunday School?

The Fellowship

The Emmanuel Baptist Church is an exciting fellowship at first glance. Members seem to be turned on to the Lord at this place; there is a climate of expectancy in the air. The well-manicured lawns emit a certain pride of ownership about the facility. The beautiful new 1.1-million-dollar sanctuary building is a model of modern architecture.

Emmanuel is a leading church in its denomination, the Southern Baptist Convention. It is a frequent state leader in baptisms, a leader in providing its pastor and staff members for leadership positions within the denomination, and a leader in terms of statistical growth. The membership of this church now exceeds 4,000, having grown from approximately 1,700 in 1977 when the Dr. Gaines assumed the pastorate. During this time, more than 800 persons have been baptized.

The founding of the Emmanuel Baptist Church goes back to August 8, 1965, when eight persons founded the congregation in the home of Mr. and Mrs. Carl Mayes in Milpitas, California. Rev. George Smith, one of the founding members, was called to pastor the church. The name *Emmanuel* was chosen from several names as the result of a drawing. It was submitted by Mrs. Isetta Mayes. By November 1965, the church had located in San Jose, California. In 1966, it joined the San Jose Baptist Association, aligned with the Southern Baptist Convention.

During Dr. George Smith's tenure, Emmanuel built an eighteen-unit apartment building known as Emmanuel Terrace for low-income, fixed-income senior citizens and disabled persons (1973). In 1977, when Dr. Gaines became pastor, the church had grown to over 1,700 members. Under his ministry it has continued the phenomenal growth rate. A significant characteristic of Emmanuel is its major emphasis on the Sunday School. One observer has commented: "Of great importance is the posture Emmanuel has taken on Sunday School and Bible study. Emmanuel prides itself with encouraging all its membership to attend various Bible studies and Sunday School classes which are held throughout the week." Out of this emphasis on Sunday School has come a large field of talented leaders who have gone on to prepare themselves for full-time Christian leadership. The church says, "The Lord has blessed Emmanuel with zestful Christians eager to do God's work. Emphasis is put on training and equipping its people to be able to win and disciple lost persons for Christ. As a result, Emmanuel has about fifteen people currently attending or who have graduated from various seminaries and Bible colleges."

This church also believes in holistic ministry to the needs of persons. They are involved in Brandon House, a home for battered women and abused children, numerous rescue missions, Christian Challenge, job assistance programs, Christian Alliance counseling, juvenile hall, San Quentin Prison, computer-aided education, and the donating of Christmas and Thanksgiving food baskets, among other ministries.

The philosophy of the church is expressed in its statement of mission purpose: "The mission purpose of Emmanuel Baptist Church is to be an extension of our Lord and Savior Jesus Christ and to continue His ministry on earth. In order to accomplish our purpose, we must press toward the mark of excellence in these three areas: 1. Go out and share the gospel with all people. 2. Care for their immediate needs. 3. Nurture them to become mature believers in Jesus Christ.

"We aim to teach and observe all things the Lord has commanded. We believe He is with us in this Great Commission to share His good news. In addition, we feel that every activity we engage in must afford all participants an opportunity to become aware of the need for a personal relationship with Jesus Christ." This commitment to the Scriptural mandates for doing the work of Christ is manifested by the fact that the rooms in the educational building of the church are named after books of the Bible.

Amos

The Dr. Willie Gaines is an imposing figure. He stands over six-feet tall and looks like a professional football player. Who is this large, appealing man who has become the first black person to be elected president of the Southern Baptist General Convention of California?

Pastor Gaines's roots go back to Saint Louis, Missouri, where he was born in 1942. He was reared in Barstow, California, where he met and married Alice M. Haley in 1960. In 1972, he graduated from Barstow College, and in 1976 he earned his bachelor of science degree from Chapman College. He is scheduled to receive his master of divinity degree from Golden Gate Baptist Theological Seminary in

1986. In recognition of his outstanding contributions to the pastoral ministry, the California Graduate School of Theology conferred an honorary doctor of divinity degree upon him in 1985.

In 1970 Gaines was called to pastor the East Barstow Baptist Church in Barstow, California. He served that congregation until 1977, when he was called to the pastorate of Emmanuel Baptist Church. In 1977 and 1978 he also served as chaplain at Almaden Air Force Station.

Pastor Gaines has been a leader in the Southern Baptist General Convention of California for a number of years. His church was in the top twenty-five in giving to missions causes through the denomination in 1984. His faithfulness earned him an invitation to serve on the Executive Board of the Southern Baptist General Convention of California. In November of 1984, the state convention elected him president. He has been a keynote speaker for a number of Southern Baptist General Convention of California events, including: the Pastors' Conference in 1979; the Woman's Missionary Union in 1981; the Dynamic Church Growth Conference in 1982; the Brothering My Brother Conference in 1982; the Singles' Conference in 1982; and in 1983 he delivered the keynote sermon at the annual convention meeting in Oakland, California. His denomination has awarded the church, under his leadership, certificates of recognition for outstanding evangelism efforts for the years 1977 through 1983. In 1981, he was a vice-chairman of the Billy Graham Crusade in California. The mayor of San Jose, California, gave him a commendation for "Excellence in Religion" in 1981.

Pastor and Mrs. Gaines have one daughter, Gaylen Marie.

The impact of the Gaines's administration at Emmanuel Baptist Church has been amazing. Since he came in 1977, membership has increased from 1,700 to over 4,000. More than 800 people have been baptized during his tenure. He has led the congregation to build a twenty-classroom educational building and a new sanctuary valued at 1.1 million dollars. Under his leadership, the church has instituted a children's ministry, a singles' ministry, an outreach ministry, new member orientation, a male chorus, two part-time staff members, two full-time staff members, and a Sunday School enrollment of over 1,100. As a result of this ministry, articles have appeared in several publications, including *Missions USA, Christian Challenge, The California Southern Baptist, Jet,* and *Ethnicity.* He is also listed in *Who's Who in America.*

What kind of preacher is Dr. Gaines? The visitor to the worship service will immediately become impressed with his communications skills. He is a very effective communicator who does it in a non-traditional way. He is not a "whooper." He is not an emotionalizer. But he is a profound, but humorous, communicator. The audience is held spellbound as he expounds from the Word of God in his folksy manner. His messages are short but deep, humorous but reverent, and simple but powerful. In his worship service, there is a sense of expectancy for the Word of God from this gifted pulpiteer. He is dynamic with dignity.

His leadership style is interesting. He does not view himself as a dictator. He is a captain of the team. He views his role as equipping the members for the performing of their ministry. He does not even sit on the platform during the worship service until it is time for him to preach. This symbolizes the sense of equality and significance of the various gifts found among the membership of the church.

Pastor Gaines does not attempt to do everything himself. He has brought together a professional staff of able persons to assist in equipping the saints for the work of the ministry. On his staff is a full-time associate minister, Rev. Elgia

Wells, with expertise in the field of religious education. A former minister of education at the church, Wells is a graduate of Golden Gate Baptist Theological Seminary. Another staffer is Mrs. Catherine Gooden, who serves as minister of education. She is in the process of completing her degree at Golden Gate in the field of religious education. One of the strengths of Pastor Gaines is to build a team with able people to assist him with leadership responsibilities.

Pastor Gaines uses a leadership style which believes in delegating responsibility to able persons in the congregation when appropriate. For example, when the new sanctuary was built, a layperson was placed in charge of the project. A report from the church described the experience like this, "An attorney by profession, Brother James Lipscomb has the implicit confidence of the pastor in his ability, so that the pastor stepped aside and delegated all responsibilities on sanctuary construction completely to him. His managerial and supervisory abilities are God's gifts to behold."

Pastor Gaines majors in doing the work of an evangelist. He is a soul-winner par excellence. He makes it a priority in his ministry to lead people to a saving knowledge of the Lord Jesus Christ. When asked how his people might describe him, his reply was: "a soul-winner."

Pastor Gaines is an outstanding pastor who has been called an example of "the new church leadership" now emerging within the Southern Baptist Convention, the largest evangelical denomination in America. His philosophy of ministry may be summed up by this statement: "Our duty is not just to preach God's love but to demonstrate that love. We are fully aware that presentation without demonstration is only conversation. We may talk about God's love all we want, but if we do not demonstrate it, it is only futile. Christ said that 'The world will know that we are His disciples by the way we show our love to one another.' Our Lord also said, 'If you love me, you will keep my commandment' (John 14:15, RSV). The die is cast and the gauntlet has been thrown. Now let us go forth boldly and show the world that we are disciples of our Lord and Savior, Jesus Christ.''

The Growing Sunday School

The Sunday School program at the Emmanuel Baptist Church has a priority. This Sunday School has grown from an average weekly attendance in 1974 of sixty to an enrollment of over 1,100 in 1985. How did this church reverse the traditional trend of apathy toward Sunday School among a predominantly black congregation? What is the story of how it was able to turn a mini-Sunday School into a mega-Sunday School?

An historical narrative from the church states the following: "In 1973 the Sunday School was reorganized under the leadership of Deacon Tom Kelly. He related he had become concerned with the lack of attendance in Bible study, so he started attending the associational conference relating to Sunday School growth. Also, Kelly visited the book store at Golden Gate Seminary and read extensively in the area pertaining to growth. His conclusion was that Southern Baptists 'had already invented the wheel, and there was no need for Emmanuel to do differently.' Kelly indicated that when he discovered Flake's Formula for Sunday School Growth,' he was impressed by the materials of the Southern Baptist Convention."

The Emmanuel Baptist Church then organized a Southern Baptist Sunday School program, and the trend began to reverse. In 1975, the church shifted its priority to emphasizing its educational ministry. Research and preliminary investigation for the construction of an educational building were initiated. The church realized that it had inadequate classroom space, but the Sunday School could still grow. Classes were held under trees and in the sanctuary. A preschool department was housed in a portable trailer. In 1977, the Rev. Gaines was called as pastor and continued the emphasis on growth through the Sunday School. In 1978, the *Life and Work Curriculum Series* was adopted under the leadership of Lymon Alexander, a deacon and Sunday School director at the church. In 1979, the church completed its new educational building which provided 10,040 square feet of educational space for the Sunday School. Also during the year, Alexander instituted outreach leaders in the adult department and attended Sunday School Week at Glorieta, New Mexico, at his own expense. He returned and led the church in an enrollment campaign through the Sunday School that resulted in an increase of 120 percent-plus over a two-year period. In 1980, Steve Warfield became the Sunday School director; under his leadership the Sunday School was led to do the following:

1. Implement weekly teachers' and officers' meetings;
2. Reorganize the Sunday School under division guidelines;
3. Implement monthly Sunday School Council planning sessions;
4. Organize a record system for the implementation of the Growth Spiral;
5. Organize a prospect file, the first for the church;
6. Adopt enrollment goals for the church year.

In 1982, Rev. Elgia Wells was called to be minister of education at Emmanuel. He continued to improve upon the emphasis in Sunday School as the result of his expertise in the field of religious education. In 1983, Rev. Kathy Gooden became minister of education, and Rev. Wells became the associate minister at the church. The church now has a goal of an enrollment of 2,000 in Sunday School by the end of 1986.

In the practice of the Emmanuel Baptist Church, the task of the Sunday School is stated:

1. To reach people for Bible study;
2. To teach the Bible;
3. To witness to persons about Christ and lead them in church membership;
4. To lead members to worship;
5. To minister to Sunday School members and non-members;
6. Interpret and undergird the work of the church and the denomination.

The organization of the Sunday School is manifested through four divisions. There is the Preschool Division which consists of boys and girls from birth until they enter the first grade. There is the Children's Division which consists of boys and girls in grades one through six. There is the Youth Division which consists of boys and girls in grades seven through twelve. There is the Adult Division which consists of men and women eighteen years of age and up. Within these divisions, the groups are divided into several categories.

In the philosophy of the Emmanuel Baptist Church: What does it take to make a successful Sunday School? Pastor Gaines answers that question in the following way. He lists five general ingredients of a successful Sunday School. First, it has a functioning Sunday School Council. The Sunday School Council exists for planning and evaluation of the Sunday School. It meets at least once a month to evaluate past records and projects. It checks progress on projects underway and plans upcoming projects and programs. Second, it practices annual promotion. It promotes people from class to class as it recognizes the natural laws of growth and development. The church believes it is a necessary factor in the normal, healthy growth of a Sunday School. Third, Sunday School workers must be of high caliber. Some qualities and characteristics of a Sunday School worker as outlined by Dr. Gaines are:

1. Motivated by a sense of calling;
2. Understands the task;
3. Commitment to the task;
4. Has integrity and self-understanding;
5. Is prepared;
6. Is enthusiastic;
7. Delegates responsibility;
8. Is faithful;
9. Seeks and follows the guidance of the Holy Spirit;
10. Loves all people.

A fourth ingredient for a successful Sunday School, according to Dr. Gaines, is to keep the Sunday School workers motivated. He suggests the following as important components of motivating the workers:

1. Set a good example;
2. Emphasize competence;
3. Practice enthusiasm;
4. Provide commendation;
5. Practice consistency;
6. Work through teamwork;
7. Set goals;
8. Do follow-up;
9. Demonstrate love.

A fifth ingredient for a growing Sunday School, according to Dr. Gaines, is having a meaningful Weekly Workers' Meeting. The Weekly Workers' Meeting provides strength and planning opportunities for the workers in the Sunday School. The good Weekly Workers' Meeting provides opportunities to pray for the Sunday School. Fellowship is generated. A sense of building team spirit is promoted. Commitment is deepened by interaction with committed peers. Correlation of programming and emphases can be carried out. Promotion of the Sunday School can be done. Planning for the Sunday School program can be maximized in this arrangement. The Weekly Workers' Meeting is so important at Emmanuel that its workers are required to commit themselves to attending at least 75 percent of the meetings.

The observer of Sunday School at the Emmanuel Baptist Church will discover several distinctive characteristics:

This is a church committed to growing through the Sunday School. It believes in the Sunday School as an effective way to reach people for the Lord. In this church the pastor sees the Sunday School as the most essential learning institution of the church.

The Sunday School at Emmanuel has a well-oiled outreach program. It has a well-developed prospect file and endeavors to enlist the prospects into the church through the Sunday School.

This church is not hesitant to establish periodically new Sunday School classes and departments. They use the Southern Baptist system of the Growth Spiral. They have discovered that the adding of new units tends to promote growth in a more consistent manner. They have discovered that new units tend to grow faster than older ones. They are not reluctant to start a new class when it is needed.

High-caliber training is provided for the Sunday School workers. Workshops at the church, training events, and denominational training opportunities are participated in by the workers of this Sunday School. They realize that thorough training is a must for an effective Sunday School, and they do not hesitate to encourage their people to go to where the information may be found.

This Sunday School understands the advantage of having adequate space for Sunday School teaching. They have recently built a new facility to provide more educational space. They understand the necessity for having adequate teacher-student ratios, and they are committed to providing the optimal learning environment for people who attend their Sunday School.

Visitation is done through the Sunday School. A systematic plan is utilized to visit prospects, absentees, and those in need of evangelistic visits. On one occasion they had a goal of knocking on five thousand doors to reach people for the Sunday School.

The curriculum at this Sunday School is Bible centered. This is a bibliocentric church. They believe in helping the members to be thoroughly involved in understanding the Word of God.

"The Sunday School has grown through the dedicated leadership of three deacons since 1974. Each has been committed to growth and effective Bible teaching. Southern Baptist materials, as well as suggested methodology for reaching people for Bible study, have been utilized. The thing that has caused our tremendous growth has been our emphasis on the Southern Baptist Sunday School."

3

Mission of
Faith Baptist Church
Chicago, Illinois
Dr. Eugene Gibson, Pastor

The Windy Community

The chill of the Chicago wind penetrates to the bone. The private world of the northern community is reflected by the well-wrapped people who travel through the streets. The tightly knit houses betray the scarcity of land in this concrete jungle. In the midst of it all, the white Gothic structure in the middle of the block stands as a symbol of God's presence amid urban humanity. This is the building of the Mission of Faith Baptist Church in Chicago.

The Mission of Faith Baptist Church is located in the Roseland-Pullman area. This lower middle-class community of approximately 62,000 stands as a memorial to the business genius of the late George Pullman who started his business nearby. Although the community is predominantly black, it is still racially mixed. Its inhabitants are mostly blue-collar workers with a mixture of professionals. The anonymity of the city permeates the area. The privacy of urbanity reflects the almost secrecy of the city life-style. The casual observer notices that in the privacy of urbania there is no shortage of an emphasis on religion. Many churches dart the blocks in this community. For example, in one two-block area there are at least seven churches. Religion is alive and well in this Chicago suburb.

The Mission of Faith Baptist Church is an exceptional church although its membership is not extremely large by comparative standards. It is a church with a membership of approximately 450. It has a Sunday School enrollment of 430! In a day when the strongest Sunday Schools tend to attract only 50 to 60 percent of a resident church membership for enrollment, the Mission of Faith Baptist Church manages to attract 90 percent-plus in Sunday School. How does this urban church do it? How does this mostly black congregation manage to become the exception and develop such an effective Sunday School enrollment program?

The Fellowship of Faith

The roots of the Mission of Faith Baptist Church go back to 1977 and Rev. Eugene Gibson. Pastor Gibson is a man of tremendous ability and has had an outstanding track record in business. Charles Chaney, in his book *Church Planting at the End of the Twentieth Century*, relates the following account of the starting of Mission of Faith Baptist Church: "Gibson worked for a number of years for Spiegel, Inc., in management. He was bumped when Spiegel merged with a larger company; and he went to work for Chicago City College, and developed a job survival curriculum for that school. Although he was pastor of a church, he didn't feel that he was accomplishing much. Then he was struck down by a heart attack which required a triple bypass operation. During convalescence, he felt a call from God to develop a black church that would be, as he says 'based on faith and a strong Bible teaching program.' The Bible teaching program in black Baptist churches has typically been weak, and the black pastors are very concerned about this. After Gibson's convalescence, he resigned as pastor and started a new church in a funeral home. This new church became the

Mission of Faith Baptist Church in Chicago, Illinois. Today it is a very thriving, agressive, ministering church in the midst of an urban society."

Early in its life, this new church demonstrated unusual abilities. With only seventy-two members at the time of its founding, the church was able to raise $30,000 within seven months. With emphasis on Sunday School and evangelism, this congregation has grown to approximately 450 members and averages about fifty to sixty baptisms per year.

Like others in this book, this strong young church believes in a holistic ministry to individuals. It is not content to sit within the walls of its beautiful sanctuary and minister only to the traditional spiritual needs of people. It believes in ministering to the total personality. This concept of ministry can be found in the ministries operated by the church. For example, the church is involved in a broadcast ministry, a ministry to nursing homes, a jail ministry, a food pantry ministry, a birthday club ministry for crisis ministries, youth job corp programs for forty to sixty young people during the summer, a senior citizens handicapped program which has been funded by federal grants, a Christian service brigade for young people, and several other types of Christian social ministries. The congregation has outgrown its present facility and is now in the process of planning to move to another location.

Pound for pound, this is one of the strongest churches in the community.

The Leader

The founder and leader of the Mission of Faith Baptist Church is Rev. Eugene Gibson, Sr. He is a large, well-built man with a winsome personality and a warm smile. Pastor Gibson was born in Chicago in 1935 but was reared part-time in Detroit, Michigan. He graduated from high school in Chicago where he was the captain of the basketball team. After graduation from high school, he attended Chicago Teacher's College. In 1969 he graduated from Moody Bible Institute with a bachelor of religious education degree and earned his master of theology degree from the International Bible Institute and Seminary. He is also a graduate of the Worsham College of Mortuary Science.

He has done graduate work at the University of Chicago and plans to enroll in the Chicago Theological Seminary to earn his doctor of ministry degree. In 1975, the Easonian Baptist Seminary awarded him the honorary doctor of divinity degree. He married Mildred Scott of York, Pennsylvania, and they are the parents of two children, Eugene and Eugenia.

Professionally, in addition to the ministry, Dr. Gibson has been the owner of a funeral home and was the first black department manager for Spiegel, Inc. He has been a department supervisor and section supervisor for data processing.

Dr. Gibson led his church into membership with the Southern Baptist Convention. During this time, he has experienced a meteoric rise to leadership within the state convention. In 1984 he was elected president of the State Ministers' Conference for the Illinois Convention which represents approximately 1,300 ministers. He was the moderator of the Chicago Metropolitan Southern Baptist Association from 1981 through 1983. The association consists of 131 churches worshipping in seventeen different languages. He is a member of the state board of directors of the Illinois Baptist State Association. He is a Sunday School consultant for the state convention and the Baptist Sunday School Board. His expertise in Sunday School work is recognized by the fact that he is the assistant Sunday School director in his association and a member of ASSISTeam. The Foreign Mission Board of the Southern Baptist Convention also has enlisted him to be an area representative.

In addition to his denominational ties, Dr. Gibson is involved in his community. He serves as president of the Roseland Clergy Association, a board member of the Council of Black Churches, a member of the New Chicago Ethics Community, and a board member of Evangelism on Campus at Kennedy-King College, a chaplain at Roseland Hospital, and a faculty member at Chicago Baptist Institute.

His philosophy is that the church and the pastor ought to be involved in the total life of the community, bringing a witness for Jesus Christ.

What kind of person is Pastor Gibson? A survey of some members of his congregation who work with him closely reveals the following impressions of him.

He is considered a strong teacher. He is well trained in Bible teaching and demonstrates great ability in sharing with others what he knows. He has earned diplomas in the area of Sunday School leadership for general officers in Sunday School and Sunday School leadership for adult leaders in Sunday School. He has also earned the MasterLife Leadership I diploma and the MasterLife Leadership II diploma. These diplomas are given by the SBC Sunday School Board for those having met minimal requirements in certain training programs. At the top of the list of what those interviewed think about him is the word *teacher.*

Pastor Gibson has unusual abilities as a leader-organizer. He has a vision of what can be and knows what steps to take in order to make that vision a reality. Many organizations have come into being as a result of his leadership and organizational ability.

He is viewed as being steadfast and faithful. He obviously

presents a strong image of consistency in the Christian faith. Perhaps this key to his personality is reflected through the name of the church, Mission of Faith.

"Excellent speaker" is a term used to describe the pastor of the Mission of Faith Baptist Church. He is an able pulpiteer. His bittersweet voice can electrify an audience. The profundity of his messages feeds the flock on Sunday morning. To hear him preach is to grow in the Lord.

Concern and compassion permeate the personality of this gifted pastor. He exudes warmth and caring. People find it easy to confide in him because they believe he really cares about them. He tries to demonstrate the love of Jesus Christ as he relates to people.

Dr. Gibson is very studious. He attempts to keep abreast of contemporary developments in theology and sociology. He believes in educating himself to keep up with what is going on in the church world. He believes that he needs to be equipped to give his members the best of his Christian experience. Therefore, he finds himself being persistent in this pursuit.

Pastor Gibson bubbles with energy, always on the go, with no hint of reluctance to do God's will about his personality anywhere. He is totally consumed by his dedication to doing the Lord's work.

This man of God is viewed as being diligent when it comes to seeking the Lord's guidance. His members say, "He seeks the Lord's guidance in everything."

In addition to the above, Dr. Gibson has been described as the following: prayerful, a great husband and father, spiritually strong, stubborn in the right way, a friend, and a hard worker.

Gibson is a musically talented pastor with an orchestra in his throat and a symphony in his mind. He has written several songs and rearranged almost one hundred others. The music program in his church is effective and qualitative.

Growth Through the Sunday School

The Sunday School enrollment at Mission of Faith is amazing! The church has more than 90 percent of its members enrolled in Sunday School. This is miraculous for any church, black or otherwise. What explains this maximum kind of enrollment in Sunday School? From the point of view of the pastor, how does a church go about getting most of its members to become enrolled in Sunday School?

The basic tool for Sunday School enrollment at Mission of Faith is the Southern Baptist Sunday School program. This body of information and collection of programs, when put together, are effective in this situation. The testimony of the pastor is this, "The Southern Baptist Sunday School program is one of the greatest tools for evangelism that I've experienced since I became a Christian. It was so effective for us that we became the first church in the seventy-five-year history of the Illinois Baptist State Association to earn the Standard Sunday School Recognition Award for outstanding Sunday School development. The nine basics of Sunday School growth when taken together are almost a guarantee that any Sunday School will grow." Again, of this particular approach to Sunday School growth, he declares, "We wouldn't want to live without it."

Qualitatively, the Sunday School program at Mission of Faith is one of the strongest in the nation. Dr. Gibson is bubbling with ideas as it relates to suggestions for building a dynamic Sunday School program. Some suggestions for growing a dynamic Sunday School include the following:

Be committed to growing through the Sunday School. Without the commitment on the part of the church, the pastor, and Sunday School workers, the Sunday School will not grow. A casual approach to the Sunday School does not result in the maxi-Sunday School. It results in the mini-Sunday School.

Emphasize enrolling church members first. Every member of the church should be expected to be enrolled in the Sunday School. Adults as well as children are expected to participate. Sunday School is not for children only. It is not for that small remnant of the church membership that happens to have an unusual interest in Bible study. Rather, it is for the whole family of the church.

Focus on enrolling new members. The church must desire to reach new people for the Sunday School. It cannot be content with merely keeping the persons it already has. It must be willing and eager to go out and enlist new people.

Use a People Search. A People Search is a systematic program to discover prospects for Sunday School and the church. This program which is sponsored by the denomination is one that has proven extremely effective in identifying and locating potential members of the Sunday School.

Use instant enrollment procedures. One of the worst handicaps of traditional Sunday Schools is that they wait until new persons attend before they enroll them. However, an alternative exists through the process of instant enrollment. This simply means that persons can be enrolled in Sunday School wherever they may be. They may be at home, at work, at school, or any other place. The Sunday School should be prepared to enroll them where they are. Keep an up-to-date prospect file. A prospect file contains the names of persons who have been identified as potential members of the Sunday School. A church should keep this prospect file up to date. It should keep a number of prospects in the file that is equivalent to the number of persons already enrolled in the Sunday School. Without this prospect file, it would be most difficult to have a meaningful visitation program.

Practice constant contact consciousness. Constant contact consciousness means being on call for a Sunday School enlistment wherever we are. It means that as we live our lives during the week, we are on call for contacting people for involvement in Sunday School. It means that we live a lifestyle which includes the awareness of our need to reach people for Sunday School.

The pastor must lead. Unless the pastor is totally committed to growing the church through the Sunday School, it will not happen. The most important person in determining the growth of a Sunday School is the pastor. He must not assign this responsibility to anyone else. If he is not interested, the Sunday School will have minimal growth.

Provide first-rate teacher training opportunities. Teachers in the Sunday School must be well trained. They need to understand how to fulfill the functions of their work. They must learn how to make the Sunday School lesson interesting; they must understand good teaching procedures; they must be aware of the resources available to make the Sunday-morning experience extremely exciting. A church has the responsibility to guarantee that a student will have a quality experience in a Sunday School class each Sunday morning.

Motivate teachers to earn diplomas. There are many training diplomas available for teachers to earn. Each diploma requires that the Sunday School teacher develop a certain level of competence in a given area. This will enable them to have the proper equipment to be effective. A goal of every Sunday School program should be to encourage each teacher to earn a maximum amount of training diplomas.

Conduct Weekly Workers' Meetings. The Weekly Workers' Meetings are extremely important in terms of planning for the next Sunday's lessons. This is a time of planning and fellowship, of reflection and review, of information and inspiration, of coordination and motivation. The Sunday

School that does not have a qualitative Weekly Workers' Meeting cripples itself as it attempts to do its task.

Conduct seminars on teacher training. From time to time the church can conduct training sessions for teachers. This provides an opportunity for new teachers to be trained, as well as for old ones to be retrained. The training experience of the faculty in a Sunday School needs to be ever-broadening. By providing seminars and workshops on teacher training, the teaching staff can be vastly strengthened.

Maintain a good record-keeping system. The reason many Sunday Schools do not grow is that they do not have records through which to measure themselves or to indicate areas of need. A good record-keeping system is very easy to establish and maintain. Every Sunday School should have a first-rate record-keeping system.

Involve new members. When a member joins a church, he or she should be immediately enrolled in the Sunday School. This practice of immediate involvement of the new members in Sunday School makes it easy for them to become a part of the church's mind-set that says: "Sunday School is one of our priorities, and every member is expected to participate."

Practice bringing somebody to Sunday School each Sunday. The members of the Sunday School should be encouraged to bring somebody else to Sunday School. Being unconcerned about bringing somebody else to Sunday School works counter to growing a Sunday School. However, when new persons come, the chances of enrolling them in the Sunday School programs greatly increase.

Use the Vacation Bible School Transfer Plan. This means that when persons enroll in Vacation Bible School, if they are not already enrolled in Sunday School, they should be transferred to its rolls. In this way, Vacation Bible School can be a powerful feeder to the Sunday School rolls. It can also be a means of identifying people who are prospects for Sunday School.

Recognize teachers for doing outstanding work. Teacher recognition goes a long way toward providing first-rate motivation for continued hard work. A church may have a Sunday School banquet at which teachers are recognized. There may be an award for the "Teacher of the Month" or the "Teacher of the Year." The idea is to encourage people who have done a good job and to motivate them and others to continue doing better.

Send Sunday School workers to outstanding national training centers in Sunday School work. For example, the Southern Baptist Convention has a national conference center at Glorieta, New Mexico, and one at Ridgecrest, North Carolina. Each summer, leading persons in the area of Sunday School work conduct workshops and seminars on the latest in Sunday School methodology. Members from churches and Sunday School workers have experienced fantastic growth as a result of being exposed to leaders in Sunday School growth. Sunday School workers can benefit by attending these seminars and workshops at the conference centers.

Promote the Sunday School from the pulpit. If the pastor promotes it from the pulpit, this will give Bible study a high degree of importance in the minds of the members. There is no more powerful promotion locus in the church than the pulpit, so the Sunday School should be promoted from the pulpit by the pastor.

Teach the Bible to win people to and to grow people in the Lord. Sound, Bible-based literature (like that available from the Baptist Sunday School Board) is needed, but the basic curriculum of the Sunday School should first be the Bible, and the basic approach should be to bring people into a saving knowledge of Jesus Christ as Lord and Savior. Nothing will help grow a Sunday School better than that emphasis.

Pastor Gibson is sold on the strategic place of Sunday School in the life of the church. He believes it ought to have priority status in the program of the church, and he feels it is absolutely essential for the ongoing of a strong church. In fact, he testifies, "To me, without the Sunday School I do not feel that a church may grow and maintain its level of growth."

4

St. Stephen Baptist Church
La Puente, California
Rev. E. W. McCall, Pastor

View

The Southern California smog burns the eyes as one turns the corner onto Walnut Avenue in the Los Angeles suburb of La Puente, California. A feeling of calmness permeates this middle-class neighborhood. This community of urbanites is a part of the megalopolis of the Greater Los Angeles area.

The prosperity of $100,000-plus homes encircles the church that dominates the corner of Walnut Street and Francisquito Avenue. The huge, modern structure revealing an imposing sanctuary and beautiful educational facilities makes a stunning impact on the onlookers. This is the church building of the St. Stephen Baptist Church in La Puente, California.

The St. Stephen Baptist Church is one of the fastest-growing churches in California. It has grown from a membership of 35 in 1970 to a congregation in excess of 2,000 today. Its Sunday School is one of the largest in the state. With its enrollment of in excess of 1,100, it stands as one of the flag bearers for effective Sunday School growth today.

How does this mostly black multiracial congregation manage to involve so many people in Sunday School? How does it successfully challenge the almost axiomatic statement that indicates blacks will not go to Sunday School? How has this church been virtually able to work a miracle in the area of Sunday School enlistment?

Genesis

The idea for the planting of the St. Stephen Missionary Baptist Church germinated in the heart of Rev. Arthur Lyle, III. Lyle had a vision for starting a church in Valinda, California. In 1964, he organized the St. Stephen Missionary Baptist Church, and it met in his residence in Valinda. Lyle remained the pastor of St. Stephen until 1969. During his tenure, the church was established on a firm foundation, and the first building fund was set up at a local bank. In 1969, Rev. Waymon Walden succeeded Lyle as pastor. During the pastorate of Rev. Walden, St. Stephen Baptist Church affiliated with the Southern Baptist Convention and established close involvement with other churches in the community. After a tenure of approximately two years, Walden resigned, and the church called Rev. E. W. McCall as pastor.

Under the pastorate of Rev. McCall, the church purchased property on Walnut Street in La Puente, California. Due to rapid growth in the membership under the leadership of Dr. McCall, the church found that it had soon outgrown its new facility. By 1974, adjoining property had been purchased; in 1975 the sanctuary had been enlarged, and a structure on the newly purchased property was utilized as an educational building. The impact of the people explosion at St. Stephen Baptist Church may be seen as it relates to building-expansion planning: "As the church grew with new members, and financially, plans were made for a new structure. After the plans were completed, a warehouse facility at the corner of Walnut Street and Francisquito was leased where we could hold services until the new structure was completed. On the first Saturday in September, 1978, we closed the old building and moved into the leased facility across the street. This location made it possible to watch the new structure as it went up. On June 24, 1979 (nine months later), we moved back to our old location but into a new edifice."

As urban sprawl began to creep out into the surrounding suburbs, this church was able to meet the needs of the growing multitudes. With the combination of able, dynamic leadership and talented middle-class people in the congregation, this church was able to be a trailblazer for other churches in the area of La Puente.

With a well-rounded program of church activities, this congregation has been able to equip many people for the work of the ministry. It has attempted to become involved in a total, through-and-through ministry to its community. Some of the manifestations of ministry include the following: an extension Vacation Bible School program that has sponsored as many as ten Vacation Bible Schools during the summer; a tutorial program that provides assistance to school-age children working below grade level or who need help maintaining or exceeding grade-level achievement; a prison ministry at the Youth Training Center in Chino, California; a business and professional women's group which provides activities for youth of the church, including an annual job fair to introduce youth persons to professional career choices available; and a job bank open during the week from 9 AM to 4 PM that assists job seekers by posting and advising of job opportunities. The church has future plans to build a senior citizen's center and a day-care center. The excitement level at the church is high and is reflected in the attendance at the Sunday morning worship service. Two worship services are necessary in order to accommodate the crowds.

The St. Stephen church is representative of a new breed of black Baptist congregations. It is characterized by able pastoral leadership, progressive denominational involvement, and the utilization of the gifts and resources of dedicated laypersons.

The Pastor

The period of rapid growth and expansion at St. Stephen Baptist Church has taken place under the ministry of Dr. E. Wilbert McCall, Sr. Dr. McCall has been able to bring together the right combination of dynamics, both spiritual and natural, to make the church into one of the leading churches in the state. Under his leadership, St. Stephen Baptist Church is a church on the move, in the process of accomplishing great things.

Who is this Joshua that leads the modern army of God in La Puente? What history does he bring?

Pastor McCall is a native of Louisiana and a graduate of Grambling State University. He received his seminary training at the American Baptist Seminary of the West where he earned the master of divinity degree and the doctor of ministry degree. While in seminary, he won the Jessie Day Drexler Scholarship Award in Pastoral Ministries. This former school teacher is active in the Los Angeles Southern Baptist Association, where he is director of church planning and a member of the finance committee. He is also active in a wide variety of denominational affairs within the Southern Baptist Convention.

Pastor McCall is tall and slender with handsome features and a quiet dignity about his person. He is well dressed with conservative styles and fits the image of a successful businessman. His warm personality portrays one who is serious about the Lord's work. His style is that of a no-nonsense businessman who is goal-directed and success-oriented. He is an achiever and who has a strategy for getting things done.

In the pulpit, he is an engaging orator. His preaching style combines the best of the able pulpiteer from the black Baptist tradition and the articulateness of the young, black urban professional. His style is dynamic, and he easily holds the attention of his audience. A man who majors on expository preaching, he is a skillful interpreter of the Word of God. Not only does he have illumination from the Word of God, but he delivers it in such a way that the members of the audience can feel it. His forceful preaching style, combined with the bittersweet sound of the Southern preacher's voice, can enable him to electrify his audience on many occasions. He is not a simple emotionalizer but one whose profound messages help build the lines of his flock.

Dr. McCall has a certain presence about his personality when he walks into the pulpit. It is as if a message is emitted, saying: "He who is in charge has arrived." In other words, "God's man" has arrived. This type of charisma enables him to have strong leadership of the flock he shepherds. One result of this charisma is his being in charge of a pulpit which is well respected.

When one is around Dr. McCall, it is easy to discover he believes in education. He believes in secular education, as revealed by the fact of his career in that area, but he is also sold on religious education, as manifested by the fact he has led his church to enroll over 1,100 in Sunday School. This brilliant man with an outstanding education is one who believes in providing a quality experience for those who sit under his ministry. In a day when the superficial is popular in many pulpits, Dr. McCall majors on the profound through the medium of religious education.

Dr. McCall has the social conscience of a modern-day Amos. Many times, particularly in his denomination, he has been the voice of conscience on selected issues of social concern. He has the courage and the vocabulary to state his case persuasively and convincingly. He is not intimated by the system, and he believes in speaking out for the right.

Rev. McCall is an outstanding pastor of this growing congregation. One of his greatest strengths is in the area of church administration. Known as an excellent administrator, he also knows how to lead his people constructively in order to motivate them to do what God wants. His sense of judgment is of the highest caliber; his sense of timing is sprinkled with wisdom. His knowledge of human nature reveals a deep understanding of what is in humankind. His command of the modern tools of administration enables him to lead a contemporary congregation of well-educated persons. His sense of prophetic vision enables him to see where the church ought to go and then provides him with the wisdom as to which alternative is the best strategy to help them achieve the goal.

In summary, Dr. E. W. McCall is a representative of the new breed of clergy within the Southern Baptist Convention. He is a progressive, young, well-educated, and skillful leader whose life is blessed with integrity and tremendous administrative acumen. His church characterizes him as a pastor concerned for all people of all ages under his guidance.

McCall and his wife, Velma, have three children—Priscilla, Wilbert, Jr., and Yolanda.

Sunday School Explosion

On Sunday morning at 9:30 AM the attractive building at 720 North Walnut Street in La Puente, California, is a maze of activity. The Sunday School starts promptly, and hundreds of people come in to participate in a thrilling Bible study program. What is this Sunday School like? What kind of organization is able to attract so many for Bible study participation on Sunday mornings?

The Sunday School at St. Stephen Baptist Church uses the Southern Baptist Sunday School program and literature. Its workers are involved in constantly improving their expertise by participating in study courses that lead to training awards in Sunday School work. During the last year, twenty-seven workers earned training awards for Sunday School improvement. This Sunday School has approximately 100 workers. The church baptized 108 persons last year with approximately 50 percent of those reached through the Sunday School.

The Sunday School has twenty-one classes and eighteen classrooms. The school keeps an up-to-date prospect file and believes in starting new Sunday School classes regularly. Audiovisual aids are used in teaching, and weekly visitation is a top priority of the program. Among the Sunday School officers are: a Sunday School director, secretary, outreach director, director of teacher training and improvement, activities director, division director, department director, teachers, outreach leaders, and group leaders. The pastor believes it is vital that he be involved in the Sunday School. While he personally does not teach a class, he does visit the different classes regularly to provide support and encouragement.

At St. Stephen Baptist Church, the Sunday School plays a major role in the growth of the church. In fact, the Sunday School is the key strategy for growing the church. According to Jacquelyn Broughton, outreach director for the Sunday School, "Sunday School plays the most important role in the growth of any church. Sunday morning Bible study prepares a person and arouses his curiosity for more of the Word. It is a small group which enables a person to get to know the church and its members. The Sunday School is the backbone of the church, contributing to its growth."

The Sunday School can have an appreciable impact on the members of a church. It can make the difference in whether or not they are well integrated into the membership. It can also make the difference in whether or not they are well educated in the Word of God. Mary Randolph is the Sunday School director at St. Stephen, and she sees the role of the Sunday School as it relates to the growth of the church serving the following: it enables the members of the body of Christ to help one another learn the truths of God's Word; it helps members experience the real, caring fellowship of ministering to one another; it provides a channel for the Sunday School members to reach out to unbelievers and share the gospel of Jesus Christ. For a church to grow both qualitatively and quantitatively, a dynamic, viable Sunday School program can make the difference.

The Sunday School program at St. Stephen has experienced phenomenal growth! Within the last five years it has grown from an enrollment of 450 to over 1,100. What are some of the reasons for this marvelous growth? Andrew Collins, assistant director of the Sunday School, lists five reasons for experiencing this growth: (1) the dedication of the workers; (2) the love and concern of each worker; (3) the outreach and inreach programs; (4) the training programs; (5) the weekly preparation and Weekly Workers' Meeting. Implicit in the above is the idea that a growing Sunday School does not merely happen. It has to be programmed, and there are successful avenues of programming this reality.

How was this church able to build a growing, dynamic Sunday School? The most important ingredient in the growth of this Sunday School was the leadership role of the pastor. In fact, the outreach director states, "Our Sunday

School has grown because of a concerned and dedicated pastor. If the pastor does not show concern, the members will feel this matter is not important. An involved pastor is most important." Dr. McCall believes in the Sunday School program. He has been featured in videotapes on Sunday School growth by the Baptist Sunday School Board. When asked why his Sunday School grows, his response is, "The Southern Baptist Sunday School materials and the proper training to use these resources are the main reasons for the constant growth in our Sunday School. With an enrollment of over 1,100 and a membership of over 2,000, we at St. Stephen Baptist Church will use no other materials for our Sunday School program."

When asked to list ten reasons why his Sunday School grows, the response of Dr. McCall was as follows:

"We use the Southern Baptist Sunday School program. We find it is very effective in our church. We believe that this Sunday School program, which is based on tried and tested principles, is the most effective way to do Sunday School in the church today. The fact that twelve other denominations use it attests to its workability.

"We use Southern Baptist Sunday School materials. We find that the Southern Baptist Sunday School materials are very effective in our setting, and that they are well-written by a group of well-trained individuals. They stimulate interest on the part of our Sunday School participants. With adaptation to our situation, we discover that we have a very potent tool to help us to reach people and keep people for Bible study.

"We involve our workers in the training offered by the Sunday School Board of the Southern Baptist Convention and local training opportunities provided by the denomination. We send our workers to the places where they can get first-rate training. For example, we have

sent as many as twenty-three workers to the National Conference Center at Glorieta, New Mexico, to sit under the teaching of some of the leading authorities on Sunday School work in our generation. Our people have come back excited and well equipped to be effective Sunday School workers at St. Stephen.

"We get involved in outreach work. We do not sit back and wait for people to come to Sunday School. We go out and get them. We believe that a Sunday School cannot grow unless it has an effective outreach program. We must go out and seek to involve people in the Sunday School program. We have an outreach program here that operates through the Sunday School, and we find this a very effective tool for reaching new people for the church and the Sunday School.

"We believe that the pastor's involvement in the total structure of the Sunday School is extremely important. I am a pastor who believes in Sunday School. I am one who believes that the pastor ought to take the lead in the Sunday School. The pastor is the leading legitimizer and validator in a church. If his body language does not say to the congregation that Sunday School is important, they will come to believe that it is not important. Therefore, there is no substitute for the deep involvement of a pastor in the Sunday School if it wishes to grow.

"First-rate teacher training and improvement classes need to be held. We believe that if people come to Sunday School, they ought to have a first-class experience while they're there. This can only happen if the teachers have been sufficiently trained to make the lesson interesting, informative, worthwhile, and inviting. We train our teachers to make sure they are competent in their areas of expertise.

"Wednesday night teachers' meeting is a very important event in our church. All of our Sunday School workers are expected to participate in the workers' meeting every week. This pro-

vides an opportunity for strengthening each other, planning for the next Sunday, and preparation for doing high-quality Sunday School work. We discover that nothing is more important than this time of planning, sharing, and fellowshipping together.

"We have a well-trained Sunday School director. At St. Stephen our Sunday School director is one who has received much training in the area of Sunday School work. She has attended many workshops and seminars. She is a mature Christian with expertise in the area of Sunday School work. The burden is lifted from the pastor when he has able laypersons trained to be able to implement the program without its losing quality. We are fortunate to have a well-trained Sunday School director at St. Stephen Baptist Church.

"We believe in well-trained teachers and support teams. We believe that teachers are called upon to provide the best of their service for the Lord. We support them through various methodologies. We believe that a teacher makes the difference in whether or not a class will thrive. So we help them to become well-trained in their duties.

"We believe that the church should be supportive of the Sunday School work. The church should offer prayerful and financial support of the Sunday School. In addition, the members of the congregation should participate. We believe that this combination will help our Sunday Schools to grow and be what the Lord would have them to be. The Sunday School does not exist as an entity by itself. It exists as a part of the church program. The church then should be 100 percent involved in support of the Sunday School program."

The Sunday School program at St. Stephen believes in practicing evangelism through the Sunday School. For example, it is not uncommon for people to accept Christ through the Sunday School. One young lady used to come to Sunday School with one of her friends, and one day she asked what must she do to become a Christian. The friend was able to point her to the Lord Jesus Christ, and she accepted Him as Lord and Savior.

The Sunday School at St. Stephen believes in ministering to the total needs of persons. There is a ministry dimension to this Sunday School experience. It is not merely a collection of people showing up to study the Bible. For example, according to the assistant Sunday School director, "One young man did not believe that his parents loved him. After he had come to Sunday School for a period of time, he inquired about how to show his love to his parents and have them respond in kind. He was told to demonstrate the love that God shows, and soon he joined the church and reported that the love between his family and himself was unbelievable." This church has a Sunday School that not only fills the mind with God's love but fills the life with solutions to problems the people of God may face.

The Sunday School at the St. Stephen Baptist Church is a super Sunday School. It has the combination of a dynamic, gifted pastor, with a vision for Sunday School, and an involved, growing laity willing to learn how to become good at doing Sunday School work.

Joe Coats spiritual leader of Glendale
Baptist Church, Miami, Florida

A view of the attractive church plant at Glendale

Willie Gaines, dynamic pastor of Emmanuel Baptist Church, San Jose, California

At Emmanuel, there is constant attention to the pupils' needs.

Learning about God's Word is superb at Emmanuel.

Eugene Gibson, God's man for Mission of
Faith Baptist Church, Chicago, Illinois

The church building of Mission of Faith Baptist Church is no doubt one of
the most beautiful edifices in the city of Chicago.

E. W. McCall, the dedicated shepherd of
St. Stephen Baptist Church, La Puente,
California

Rev. McCall and some of his leaders down front during a worship service

E. V. Hill, widely known pastor-preacher
of Mt. Zion Missionary Baptist Church,
Los Angeles, California

Going to Mt. Zion is an enjoyable experience for all ages.

The impressive Church plant of Mt. Zion Missionary Baptist Church stands on a strategic corner in Los Angeles.

Lonnie Dawson, the vibrant pastor of the New Mount Calvary Baptist Church, Los Angeles, California

Classes for youth and young adults are often taught out of doors on the church grounds of New Mount Calvary.

The church building stands as a lighthouse amid the hurry and scurry of the metropolis.

George O. McCalep, Jr., shepherd of the fast-growing flock at Greenforest Baptist Church in Decatur, Georgia

Greenforest Baptist Church believes in having the best possible facilities for its Bible-teaching program.

All kinds of carefully planned Sunday School promotions are conducted at Greenforest, including this Easter program with its culminating balloon release.

Billy Baskin, faith-inspiring pastor of the
New Way Fellowship Baptist Church,
Miami, Florida.

Here is Youth # 5 in action at New Way Fellowship.

J. Herbert Hinkle, motivational pastor of the Cathedral of Faith, Inkster, Michigan

SENIOR CITIZEN'S FASHION SHOW

The Cathedral of Faith believes in a wide range of activities to engage the interest of the community, including this fashion show.

BAPTIZING IN OUR SWIMMING POOL

Baptizing in the Cathedral of Faith swimming pool

Harold Carter, pastor of New Shiloh Baptist Church (right) is being interviewed by Sid Smith, author of *10 Super Sunday Schools in the Black Community*.

The marvelous Gothic sanctuary of the New Shiloh Baptist Church, Baltimore, Maryland.

New Shiloh makes maximum use of computers in its training and ministry.

5

Mt. Zion
Missionary Baptist Church
Los Angeles, California
Dr. E. V. Hill, Pastor

The massive, white-stucco building dominates the corner of 50th and Hooper in the heart of South Central Los Angeles. The elegant Spanish architecture accentuates the presence of this house of the Lord in the Greater Watts area of the nation's second largest city. Located in the heart of the ebony ghetto, Mount Zion Missionary Baptist Church has arms that stretch around the world. It has earned its reputation as one of "the greatest churches in America"—a designation given by *Decision* magazine.

Mt. Zion sits only a few blocks from the scene of the fatal Symbionese Liberation Army vs. Los Angeles Police Department shoot-out in the mid-70's after the kidnapping of Patricia Campbell Hearst. It also sits in the heart of the "curfew zone" implemented in 1965 to control the traumatic Watts riot—a conflagration that indelibly scarred the community. Yet it stands as a symbol of hope for thousands who feel the impact of its myriad ministries. A sign on the parking lot preaches, "A child brought up in Sunday School is rarely brought up in court." The casual observer quickly discovers that Mt. Zion has a total ministry.

Roots

What is the history of this church which has earned the designation of being one of America's great churches? How did Mt. Zion evolve from humble beginnings to greatness? What are the salient points in its story?

Mt. Zion's history is traced back to 1892. On May 12, 1892, a meeting was held on San Pedro Street in South Los Angeles, in which the church was organized with twenty-six charter members. The new church met without a pastor until October, 1892, when the Rev. Davis R. Evans accepted the call to serve as minister of the new congregation. Early actions of the church included joining the Western Baptist Association (now the Western Baptist State Convention) and incorporating for legal purposes. After being called as pastor, Evans' served four years.

In 1896, S. A. Smith succeeded Evans as pastor of Mt. Zion. In this historic year of the Supreme Court ruling in Plessy vs. Ferguson, the young church experienced difficulty of a magnitude to result in a change of pastoral leadership after only seven months.

The successor to the leadership of Smith was Rev. Sippie Thompson, a charter member of Mt. Zion. He served from 1898 to 1905 and led the church to establish physical roots in Los Angeles. For ten years Mt. Zion worshiped in several locations. Thompson led the church to purchase a mission site owned by the First Baptist Church, Los Angeles, located at Third and Traction. The property was paid for within six years during the Thompson administration.

Beginning in 1906, Mt. Zion experienced a tremendous spurt of growth in membership. Pastor Pearcy came from Louisiana to serve Mt. Zion in 1906. The combination of an attractive building and the leadership qualities of Pearcy yielded an exciting period of growth in the life of the church.

So much growth occurred that an enlargement program was implemented to accommodate a seating capacity of 1,200 worshipers during the five-year tenure of Rev. Pearcy.

In 1911, Rev. Joseph T. Hill succeeded Pastor Pearcy as minister of Mt. Zion. Joe Hill was a gifted singer and talented pulpiteer whose ministry earned Mt. Zion the reputation of "one of the greatest churches in the city." The ministry of this large congregation was expanding and impacting ever-widening circles. The pastor resigned in 1916 to expand his ministry into the area of music through singing tours.

Pastor Hill was followed by Rev. Sydney Brooks in 1917. This native of North Carolina had a short pastorate at Mt. Zion which lasted a little over a year before he resigned. Later, he organized the Progressive Baptist Church in Los Angeles.

The short tenure of Brooks was the beginning of a series of very short pastorates for the church. In 1920, Rev. Grandville Reed, a Mississippi scion of slave parentage, became pastor and served less than a year and a half. However, during the Reed pastorate the church became a significant presence in National Baptist denominationalism. In fact, Reed was elected president of the Pacific Baptist Convention and director of Christian education.

In April, 1924, the mantle of leadership was passed to Rev. Andrew Jackson Stokes. His pastorate lasted only five months before being terminated by his untimely death.

After a period of mourning, a long era of unprecedented stability was bestowed upon the church. After several short pastorates, Mt. Zion would experience continuous pastoral leadership for the next thirty years. The calling of Rev. Frank Herman Prentice in 1925 ushered in an unprecedented long tenure of able pastoral leadership. Prentice was a talented leader for the growing church. Under his leadership the church caught a vision of the financial support of foreign missions. In fact, Mt. Zion became the nation's leading giver to the Foreign Mission board of the National Baptist Convention, USA, Inc., during his pastorate. While he served the church, a new edifice was erected to seat the growing membership. During the thirty-three-year pastorate of this "great pastor, leader, and preacher," the impact of the church was great for the kingdom of God. The pastor earned two significant designations from his peers: "the Sweetheart of Foreign Missions" and "the Prince of Preachers of the National Baptist Convention." After retiring in 1958, he served as pastor emeritus until his death in 1971.

Rev. Percy Williams became pastor of Mt. Zion after the retirement of Rev. Prentice in 1958. During his two-year tenure he completed the construction of an educational building and made other improvements.

The present pastor, Dr. Edward Victor Hill, succeeded Pastor Williams in 1962. This young pastor with gifted potential would lead the church to its greatest heights. Armed with the belief that "if you have the faith, God has the power," E. V. Hill has led Mount Zion to become one of the great churches of the present generation.

Ministries of Mt. Zion

Mt. Zion Missionary Baptist Church, under the leadership of Dr. E. V. Hill, has made gargantuan strides in ministry effectiveness. In fact, so impressive are their ministries that it is almost mind boggling! Dr. Hill's philosophy permeates the mind-set of the church. He believes that New Testament churches should be characterized by four major emphases. He uses the analogy of a baseball game to describe these emphases: first base is evangelism; second base is Christian social ministries; third base is social action; and home plate is celebration. This philosophy is embraced and implemented through multitudinous ministries.

A partial listing of ministries of the Mt. Zion Missionary Baptist Church under the pastorate of Dr. Hill includes:

The World Christian Training Center

The World Christian Training Center is an evangelistic program founded and directed by Dr. Hill. Its purpose is to recruit to Christ and train at least one person in every block. With a full-time staff, the ministry of the World Christian Training Center has been directly responsible for leading more than 15,000 people to Christ, besides many others won by churches trained through its program. The ministry of the World Christian Training Center has been extremely effective. Since its inception, in excess of 6,000 people have been trained through at least 100 classes. Over 1,200 people have surveyed their block for Christ.

More than 150 prayer groups have been organized, and in excess of 100 churches now have a nucleus of workers trained by the center. The World Christian Training Center is used as a model by other evangelistic organizations. Its methods have been adopted by the California Southern Baptist Convention and the block-by-block concept has been adopted by Campus Crusade, International, to be used in some 2,400 cities throughout the world. Satellite centers are located in Cleveland, Dallas, Denver, Atlanta, Chicago, Detroit, and Brooklyn. There is also an international office of the World Christian Training Center in Seoul, Korea.

World Vision

Mt. Zion is a compassionate church as it relates to the world hunger crisis. Several thousand dollars are contributed through the humanitarian organization, World Vision, annually. Additionally, special drives have yielded such amounts as $25,000 for hunger relief through the organization. Through Mt. Zion's involvement with World Vision, homes have been rebuilt in Guatemala. The idea to rescue boat people on the China Sea was born in Pastor Hill's study during a conversation with Dr. Stanley Mooneyham.

Voice of Africa Mission

The Voice of Africa Mission is a boarding school for African students located 150 miles in the interior of Monrovia, Liberia. Mt. Zion has built a dormitory for boys, donated a herd of sheep, and provided monthly financial support for this mission.

The Foreign Mission Board of the National Baptist Convention, USA, Inc.

Mt. Zion is a leading contributor to foreign missions through the Foreign Mission Board of the National Baptist Convention, USA, Inc. In addition to systematic giving, special projects have been initiated. Two dormitories have been built in La Sota, a tractor complete with accessories was purchased by the church and shipped to Liberia, and a church for nationals has been built in South Africa.

The Foreign Mission Board of the National Baptist Convention of America

Through this mission board, Mt. Zion participates in missions by paying the tuition of forty Jamaican students per year on a quarterly basis. On a monthly basis, the church supplements the salaries of three Jamaican pastors. The congregation restored the roof of a storm-damaged church in Jamaica. These Christians also equipped the delivery room in a hospital in Liberia.

Prison Ministry

Mt. Zion's prison ministry is a joint effort between the E. Victor Fellowship Ministries of Zion, laypersons, and well-known entertainers who minister with incarcerated people at various correctional institutions in Southern California. In this ministry Bible study groups have yielded several hundred professions of faith, and scores have been placed on jobs upon release from prison.

Baptist World Alliance

The ministry of Mt. Zion extends to the worldwide body of Baptists known as the Baptist World Alliance. Mt. Zion participates in this organization through financial contributions and the direct involvement of the pastor. A few years ago the church gave $5,000 to help needy people of the world. Dr. Hill's involvement has included preaching at the Baptist World Alliance in Stockholm, Sweden, and addressing the organization's executive committee in Jamaica. He served on the Baptist World Alliance committee on reconciliation.

Liberian Baptist Convention

Mt. Zion has the distinction of being a member of a foreign convention. The church is a member of the Liberian Baptist Convention located in Liberia, West Africa, and provides annual financial support.

Released Time Education

Released Time Education, a program of the Los Angeles Board of Education in which students are released an hour per week for Bible study in churches, has been greatly supported by Mt. Zion. The church provides teachers, supervisors, assistants, classrooms, and substantial financial support for the program.

Have Gospel, Will Travel

Through this ministry the church supports a missionary and paid for the shipment of food, clothing, and medicine to missionaries in Haiti and the Philippines.

African Enterprise

African Bishop Festo Kivengere leads the African Enterprise, an evangelistic social concern ministry in Africa. African Enterprise has work in Uganda "attempting to restore that country from the destruction of Idi Amin." Mt. Zion provides yearly financial support and gives grants (one for $5,000) to this ministry. The pastor is a member of African Enterprise's Board of Reference.

Campus Crusade

Mt. Zion is an enthusiastic supporter of Campus Crusade for Christ, International. The church has involvement with the organization through the World Christian Training Center. Campus Crusade sends workers to the church for participation in witnessing programs. Dr. Hill, a frequent speaker at Campus Crusade functions nationally, is a member of the organization's Billion Dollar Campaign.

Mt. Zion Towers

Mt. Zion Towers is ministry for disabled people and/or senior citizens. This government-assisted project consists of a twelve-story, 118-apartment complex valued in excess of $5,000,000 equipped with spacious rooms equipped with appliances, bath, and other conveniences. Under the leadership of the pastor this impressive project was initiated, organized, and completed.

E. Victor Villa

E. Victor Villa is another senior-citizens and disabled-persons-related ministry generated by the church. Like Mt. Zion Towers, E. Victor Villa is an apartment complex built under the leadership of Dr. Hill. It contains forty-six apartments and is valued in excess of $1,500,000.

Speak Gospel Hands

Mt. Zion has initiated a dactylology ministry. Speak Gospel Hands is a ministry to assist persons "who cannot hear or speak or who have varying degrees of speaking and hearing ability." Through a department of the church these persons are recruited, instructed in the Christian faith, and assisted in various areas of need. At least fifty members of the church participate in this ministry to more than 100 persons. A result of Speak Gospel Hands is the generating of a state of California grant to establish a center for those who have difficulty speaking and hearing.

Women's Christian Temperence Union

In 1962, the church began its outreach ministry through the Women's Christian Temperence Union. At Mount Zion, "Women's Christian Temperence Union" is a group of Christian women banded together to promote clean living and the protection of the home. They teach family members, with a special emphasis on children, to abstain from liquor and drugs. They have year-round classes and programs highlighting each summer with a camp outing."

The S.T.E.P. Foundation

Dr. Hill was among the founders of the S.T.E.P. (Strategies to Elevate People) Foundation, an organization to develop national prototypes in designated neighborhoods in Dallas, Denver, and Los Angeles, to demonstrate effective projects to help the poor. More than 900 volunteers are involved. On the committee are Holly Coors, Mary Crowley, N. Bunker Hunt, Clint Murchison, and other prominent people. Dr. Hill serves as president.

BARAC

In 1984, Pastor Hill led Mt. Zion to contribute $25,000 to feed hungry people in Africa through the organization BARAC (Black Americans Responding to the African Crisis).

The Lord's Kitchen

A ministry to feed hungry people in Los Angeles has been initiated by Dr. Hill. A building has been purchased, and an everyday program to feed the hungry has been started.

The Fragment Center

This pastor has started a ministry to clothe needy people. A building has been purchased, and clothes are sold or donated on a needs basis.

The Hungry People Drive

Mt. Zion, under Dr. Hill's leadership, raised and donated $65,000 to hungry people through a fund-raising program called the Hungry People Drive. Members were encouraged to develop a project to raise money and donate the proceeds to the hungry.

Opportunities Industries Centers

Mt. Zion was instrumental in the founding of the Opportunities Industries Center in Los Angeles. The OIC in Los Angeles was organized by Pastor Hill with the church providing facilities, staff, and seed money of $10,000.

Through this organization, thousands have been involved in self-advancement in the labor force as a result of having been trained and motivated in the program. The impact of OIC in Los Angeles was immediate: In its first year's operation with Pastor Hill as chairman, it placed 443 people into full-time employment in six months. It received a $500,000 grant from the Ford Foundation and $1,000,000 worth of equipment from industry.

The United Benevolent Society

The United Benevolent Society, organized and directed by Dr. Hill, "is an organization of dues-paying members designed to assess the needs of its membership through benevolence and the creation of economic opportunities through group participation." It provides for members "counsel, personal assistance, group-purchasing opportunities, group-insurance opportunities, and many others." This ministry has been very productive. A report summarized its activities: "Since its inception, thousands of dollars have been saved through the group purchasing program . . . over $300,000 has been paid to the beneficiaries of members of the Society through the group insurance plan. Fifty thousand dollars has been given directly to churches in memorial of our TUBS members."

The Work Experience Program

The Work Experience Program was organized by Pastor Hill through the World Christian Training Center as a ministry to young people between the ages of sixteen and twenty-one who find themselves out of school and unemployed. This ministry has trained and placed over 400 young people in jobs. The program was made possible by a grant from the city of Los Angeles through the leadership of Mayor Bradley. The Work Experience Program has been "cited in the records of Congress as one of the most successful training programs in the United States."

The Ethiopian Call

Mt. Zion contributed $15,000 to The Ethiopian Call, an effort to establish an agricultural demonstration community in Ethiopia to promote self-sufficiency through the modern usage of agriculture.

Civil Rights Organization Involvement

This inner-city church in South Central Los Angeles is a supporter of traditional civil rights organizations such as the Urban League, National Association for the Advancement of Colored People, the Southern Christian Leadership Conference, and People United to Save Humanity. Financial support is provided, members are personally involved, and the pastor is involved in various ways.

The Pastor

Dr. E. V. Hill is the dynamic pastor of the Mount Zion Missionary Baptist Church. This charismatic leader is a big man, both in physical stature and ministry impact. If the church had "superstars," he would surely qualify as one of the brightest.

From whence came this man of God? What are some milestones of his ministry?

Edward Victor Hill is a native of Texas. He lived in a two-room log cabin in the sandy hills of Central Texas near Sweet Home. Born in the midst of the Great Depression and the "Jim Crow" era, he was introduced to this world in a climate of poverty and racism. After graduating from high school he enrolled in Prairie View A & M College where he earned a bachelor of science degree in agriculture. During this time he met and married Jane Carruthers, the daughter of the dean of the School of Agriculture.

In 1951 he accepted the call to the ministry. Greater Mt. Zion Missionary Baptist Church ordained him to the gospel ministry in 1955. Early in his ministry, young Ed Hill showed a skilled aptitude for national leadership through being elected president of the Youth Department of the National Baptist Convention in 1951. In 1954 Hill was called to his first church, Mt. Olive Baptist Church in West Austin, Texas. He served there a short time until Mt. Corinth Baptist Church in Houston invited him to serve as pastor. During his Houston pastorate, he became active in the civil rights movement and involved in the political arena. (It was E. V. Hill who nominated Martin Luther King, Jr., for president of the S.C.L.C.). After six years as pastor of the Houston church, Mt. Zion Missionary Baptist Church called him to Los Angeles in 1960.

When the new pastor arrived at Mt. Zion, he found a church in crisis. The church had split numerous times; its property notes were facing foreclosure, and $150,000 worth of law suits had been initiated against the congregation. With a swift, strong stroke of leadership, the young pastor was able to lead the church to reverse the trend of adversity. Through four major actions, the situation at Mt. Zion was turned around:

1. He immediately suspended the operation of all organizations and officers other than those which were essential;

2. He began teaching the whole church from the Bible about the function of every office and organization of the church;

3. He established and taught church conferences every Wednesday night;

4. He established and taught church school workshops every Thursday night.

After seventeen months of intense Bible study on the total operation of the church, Mt. Zion emerged as a church built on a biblical foundation. The financial status of the church improved dramatically: all property notes were paid off within six months, and all pending law suits had been settled within three months for $800!

During the first half year of his pastorate, Hill reorganized every church organization and organized thirty-two circles. He resurrected the church's involvement with former pastors of the church, denominational programs, and community movements. Within two years, the sanctuary and educational buildings had been completely refurbished and refurnished, and the church purchased two additional lots. Through the new pastor's leadership, the once-great church, known for being led by a "prince of preachers," took a giant step forward on its road to progress.

It is often noted that a church rises no higher than its pastor. Mt. Zion can expect to stand tall because its pastor stands tall. The accomplishments of Dr. E. V. Hill are not simply outstanding: they are spectacular! Space does not permit even a hint of this talented leader's contributions in this work. However, a partial listing of achievements provides a clue to his involvements:

In 1963, Dr. Hill led the church to begin supporting forty full-time students in Jamaica.

In 1964, he organized the Los Angeles OIC and led the church to purchase and ship a fully equipped tractor to Africa. Dr. Hill was appointed the first chairman of the Los Angeles Poverty Program with an $18,000,000 budget.

In 1965, he was appointed a member of the Los Angeles Housing Authority, a group of which he later became chairman. More than 1,100 units for low income people were built during his tenure. During the summer, Pastor Hill led Mt. Zion to sponsor a special program of Vacation Bible School which resulted in enrolling 905 students with 200 accepting Christ.

1966 was an impactful year for Dr. Hill's ministry. He began a radio ministry, organized The United Benevolent Society, and sponsored another Vacation Bible School program which enrolled 7,000 with 612 candidates for baptism.

In 1967, Hill organized Mt. Zion's credit union.

In 1968, he led his church to build two dormitories in Lesotho, South Africa, and to purchase ninety-nine sheep for use in Liberia.

In 1969, the pastor was named to the Los Angeles Fire Commission. Later, under his chairmanship, the problem of racial discrimination in the fire department was addressed.

In 1970, Pastor Hill founded the World Christian Training Center and organized and constructed E. Victor Villa, Inc., a senior citizens complex.

In 1971, Dr. Hill organized and erected Mt. Zion Towers, another senior citizens complex. In that year he was elected president of the California State Baptist Convention, which he served for eight years and raised $500,000 for mission, education, and evangelistic causes. The Ethiopian Call ministry was organized by Dr. Hill in 1971.

In 1972, Dr. Hill delivered a prayer at the inauguration of President Richard M. Nixon.

In 1973, he received an appointment to the Los Angeles City Planning Commission where he served as vice-chairman and received many awards for his labors on behalf of the poor in the housing area.

In 1975, Hill led the California State Baptist Convention to increase dramatically giving to the poor and to build a home in Guatemala for the needy. He also "became consul general to the Republic of Liberia in charge of all the affairs of the Republic of Liberia west of Chicago." Pastor Hill led Mt. Zion to give $23,000 for starving Africans.

In 1976, Mt. Zion participated fully in Here's Life, America, donated to the Guatemalan Building Fund, and refurbished the auditorium and educational building. The church also adopted a Vietnamese refugee couple and provided food and shelter for them for one year as they relocated in the United States.

In 1977, Pastor Hill initiated "Operation Everything," a soul-winning effort implemented through fifty-two evangelistic committees which yielded 1,103 decisions for Christ within ninety days. The Speak Gospel Hands Department was organized in the church during this year. The pastor was one of the organizers of the Baptist Joint Commission of California, composed of six state conventions with membership in excess of 1,000,000 people. He also assisted in establishing the Campus-Crusade-related Agape Training Base in South Central Los Angeles, resulting in more than 300 Agape candidates living and working among the members of the church.

In 1978, Dr. Hill led Mt. Zion to give $10,000 to purchase a portable transmitter for a Liberian mission, to sponsor an accredited summer school due to the public schools not operating, and to raise $103,000 to purchase two and one-half acres of land in the inner city. During the year Dr. Hill was selected as visiting professor at California Graduate School of Theology. Other major accomplishments included: sponsoring the first Living Proof Musical, which resulted in 117 decisions for Christ, and organizing the World Christian Training Center Work Experience Program.

In 1979, Evangelist Hill preached fourteen city-wide revivals across America and organized Oikos, "a family witnessing program designed to reach every member's family throughout the world." He traveled with Dr. Jesse Jackson to Israel, Jordan, and Lebanon "on a fact-finding tour."

In 1980, Pastor Hill was elected president of the Baptist Joint Commission of California. During his administration the Baptist Joint Prison Ministry of California was incorporated. During the political campaign, he "actively campaigned for the Republican Party platform and president, being a member of the National Roundtable and the Moral Majority."

President Ronald Reagan appointed Dr. Hill to the Committee on the Bicentennial of the US Constitution in 1985. Earlier, he was invited to chair the US Civil Rights Commission, but declined.

Five institutions of higher learning have honored this gifted pastor with an honorary doctorate in recognition of his outstanding leadership in the ministry.

In addition to the above, Dr. Hill has served or serves in the following capacities: president of S.T.E.P. (Strategies to Elevate People); member of the Presidential Task Force on Private Sector Initiatives; chairman of the National Concerned Clergy for Evangelism; chairman, Campus Crusade for Christ's Here's Life, Inner City; member of the Board of Governors of the Council on National Policy; member of the Board of Directors of Bishop College; member of the Board of Trustees of Morehouse School of Religion; member of the Board of Directors of America for Jesus.

Dr. Hill is also a member of the Board of Reference for three organizations: African Enterprise, Bob Harrison Crusades, and the Christian Embassy. He serves as a vice-president of the National Baptist Convention, USA, Inc., a convention in which he holds a life membership.

Clearly, Dr. Hill is one of the giants in the ministry today. His record makes that abundantly clear. His skills as an organizer, dreamer, builder, administrator, and politician are major-league caliber. However, his pulpit ability has been acclaimed as foremost. In 1979, *Time* magazine named him one of the seven top preachers in America. In 1984 *Ebony* featured him as one of the fifteen best black preachers in the United States.

Dr. Edward Victor Hill will go down in history as one of God's ablest servants. What is the secret of his effectiveness? Perhaps this excerpt from his "Twentieth Jubilee Luncheon Feast" program sums it up well:

Once, during an anniversary period of our pastor, a young preacher asked Pastor Hill what he should do to fall into a good thing like Mount Zion.

Pastor Hill replied, "Son, you do not fall into good things. You, by God's help and permission, work up into good things."

Then Pastor Hill said, "Why don't you try Matthew 20:4?"

In these past twenty years, Pastor Hill has received awards, plaques, honors, degrees, funds, position, and fame untold.

But also in these twenty years, he has worked, and often this has been overlooked.

The Mount Zion Sunday School

The Sunday School at Mt. Zion has an enrollment of approximately eleven hundred persons. On Sunday mornings the Sunday School is a mass of activity. The effectiveness of their Sunday School program proves that many people can be reached through this medium.

How does this church reach 60 percent of its membership for Sunday School? What are major characteristics of this mega Sunday School? The following characterizes Mt. Zion's Sunday School:

An inclusive definition of Sunday School—Mt. Zion's definition of the Sunday School is "the church in its teaching service." This definition stresses emphasis on the involvement of the whole congregation. They do not write off any group from participation. In their view Sunday School is not for children only. It is for the entire family from cradle to grave. They have been liberated from the "children's syndrome" of the mini-Sunday School. When members join the church they are expected to enroll in Sunday School. In the philosophy of this congregation Sunday School participation is not optional. Dr. Hill believes every member of Mt. Zion ought to be active in Sunday School. At Mt. Zion the Sunday School is the Bible teaching program for the entire church.

Committed leadership—The leadership of Mt. Zion is committed to the high priority of Sunday School. The pastor is not a casual supporter; he is not a passive endorser; he is not merely a reviewer of the lesson. He is not distantly detached. He is not merely the teacher of teachers only. No, he is as involved as he can be! Dr. Hill is so involved in his Sunday School that he even serves as superintendent! He maintains that there is not a more important function in the church than teaching the people, and he supervises the process personally. Therefore, the Sunday School at Mt. Zion is thoroughly permeated with the spiritual heartbeat of the pastor. It exudes his value system; it breathes his influence. Unquestionably, the pastor is the leader of the Sunday School at this church. Unquestionably, the commitment of the pastor is the key for the effective Sunday School. In fact, as Dr. Hill puts it: "The ideal pastor unites all of his vision, experiences, and aspirations with those of the membership and keeps before the church an all-inclusive program that will give every member the inspiration, and make available the information needed to have a constructive Sunday School."

A philosophy of quality standards—Mt. Zion's Sunday School has a definite philosophy about the ideal toward which it strives. In their philosophy, the ideal Sunday School is timely, has inspiring assemblies, keeps perfect report records, has a calendar of events, has a complete staff, supports the general church program, is well-graded, provides the best literature, has a well-attended and organized workers' meeting, and is represented in denominational and other informative meetings.

Qualitative Sunday School workers—At Mt. Zion those who work in Sunday School are expected to maintain high standards of service. They are expected to be good followers, timely, and knowledgeable of "every phase of the work and purpose of the Sunday School." Their ideal worker "is approachable and able to maintain a Christlike disposition under unusual circumstances." He or she is expected to be an active soul-winner and a dedicated teacher of the Bible to everyone, regardless of social status or race. Workers are expected to check with those in authority about plans, programs, and problems. They are also expected to be exemplary in support of the total church program. Not just "anything goes" relating to Sunday School workers at Mt. Zion. If one wants to be a Sunday School worker at this church, he or she must be willing to do it well.

Evangelistic emphasis—Mt. Zion is a thoroughly evangelistic church. Personal evangelism permeates every program of the church. The record of Mt. Zion is abundantly clear that this is a soul-winning church. One of the ideal characteristics of the Sunday School worker is a dedication to winning souls to Christ. Mt. Zion's Sunday School has an Evangelism Committee responsible for constantly presenting opportunities to accept Christ as Savior. This committee publicizes soul-winning efforts and distributes soul-winning materials to soul-winners and prospects alike.

It works closely with Sunday School teachers in the area of personal evangelism. It actively leads the Sunday School in creative types of outreach evangelism projects such as street meetings, rescue mission work, and other kinds of evangelistic enterprises. It is no secret that one of the great characteristics of the Sunday School of Mt. Zion is its emphasis on personal evangelism.

A Strong Emphasis on Weekly Workers Conference.—One of the strong emphases in the Mt. Zion Sunday School program is its Weekly Workers' Conference. All Sunday School workers are expected to attend. This is viewed as an important training and planning opportunity for the ongoing of the school. It is held at a time convenient for the workers, and few excuses are accepted for their nonattendance. The Weekly Workers' Conference is an event that undergirds the effectiveness of the Sunday School worker in class on Sunday. The ideal Weekly Workers' Conference schedule includes an emphasis on devotion, an emphasis on instruction, announcements and observations, studying the background and physical settings of the lesson, and remarks and encouragement from the pastor.

An Emphasis on Christian Fellowship—The Sunday School program at Mt. Zion consists of more than simply teaching the Bible. It also contains an emphasis on Christian fellowship. Included in departmental activities for the Sunday School are annual social outings, parties, suppers, picnics, and tours. The idea is to involve the members of the Sunday School class in a broad range of Christian fellowship experiences. The Sunday School is more than a place where the Bible is taught; It is also a place where Christians experience and minister to each other.

An Emphasis on Starting New Sunday Schools.—At Mt. Zion, the Sunday School is not content merely to serve those who come to the church. It holds the philosophy that it is their responsibility to go out into the community and discover places where Sunday Schools are needed. The church then will establish a new Sunday School in an area without one. Sometimes they refer to these as mission Sunday Schools and provide the personnel to organize a new Sunday School and start it. One such Sunday School is held at a housing project in the greater Watts area of Los Angeles. This Sunday School believes in starting new Sunday Schools as a way to reach more people.

An Emphasis on Holistic Ministry.—The Sunday School at Mt. Zion emphasizes ministering to the total needs of persons. It does not believe that human beings can be segmentalized and sufficiently enjoy the whole ministry of the church. The Sunday School, therefore, involves its members in various types of ministry. Some of these ministries include the following: an athletic program, a sick visitation program, a mission program, a temperance campaign, an evangelistic campaign, a doctrinal study campaign, and study courses on various aspects of the life of the church. The philosophy at Mt. Zion is: the church ought to minister to the total needs of the individual, and so should its Sunday School.

A Well-Defined Organizational Structure.—There is no doubt about what the Sunday School expects at Mt. Zion. The entire program is well defined and well structured in order to meet the needs of the people. When persons become involved in the Sunday School program, a manual is given to them that contains detailed descriptions of ideas for Sunday School work in the church. There is a definition for the ideal Sunday School class, class procedure, class officers and their duties, weekday activities, the ideal teacher, ideal teacher's equipment, ideal preparation steps, ideal steps to be taken in sharing the lesson, a lesson plan for teachers and workers, the ideal reporting system, the ideal general report, the ideal departmental report, the ideal class reports, the ideal student report, and examples of ideal songs for use in Sunday School. This Sunday School is organized and knows where it is going, and that is shared with each new worker.

A Carefully Selected Teaching Staff.—Great care is taken in the selection of teachers for the Sunday School at Mt. Zion. Ideally, each teacher has a sense of calling to serve in the capacity of working in the Sunday School. From the point of view of the church, "The ideal teacher has a sense of calling to the teaching ministry of Christ; the ideal teacher is able to persuasively and effectively present the Word of God." So a teacher is not simply someone who is able to be persuaded to fulfill the function but a person who has concluded that God has called him or her to serve in that capacity. Teachers are expected to view themselves as "workmen in God's workshop." The teacher should have divine motives and spiritual goals. From the vantage point of the church, a teacher must be able to excuse self and desire to see fruits from his/her labor. Each teacher is expected to bring a message to the class. When the teacher appears in class, there is the expectation that he or she does so under the influence of the Holy Spirit. The teacher is expected to challenge the class and demonstrate some evidence of the power of the Word of God. At Mount Zion, each teacher has three binding obligations: to be something, to know something, and to share something.

A Well-prepared Teaching Staff.—The anachronism of the unprepared teacher is not apparent at Mt. Zion. Each teacher is expected to be well prepared for the presentation of the Sunday School lesson. Training is given in detail to ensure that teachers are abundantly prepared for their task. They are encouraged to utilize equipment in preparation for the delivery of the lesson.

Some equipment used includes the following: the Bible, a dictionary, a Bible dictionary, a concordance, commentaries, maps, a teacher's quarterly, and a pupil's quarterly. Each teacher is encouraged to read the lesson through, reread the lesson, and study the lesson before he or she attempts to teach it. The lesson should be bathed in prayer and envisioned in detail before being taught on Sunday morning. In fact, it is stressed that the lesson must become a fixed vision in the mind of the teacher, so it can be clearly seen as it relates to the aims, purposes, and needs that it will fulfill. Finally, each teacher must be prepared to extend an evangelistic invitation during the Sunday School class period.

Summary

The phenomenal Sunday School at Mount Zion is almost breathtaking in a day when it is extremely difficult to induce many people in the black community to attend Sunday School. Mt. Zion seems to have found an effective combination to enlist members and prospects in Sunday School. How do they do it? Many factors are involved. The pastor is the leader and the one who inspires the vision for the great Sunday School. Prayerful care is taken in enlisting and selecting of workers. High standards are expected of those who agree to participate in the Sunday School as leaders. Training opportunities are offered for those who have indicated a desire to serve. The Sunday School is viewed as an evangelistic tool for teaching the lost. It focuses on teaching the Word of God. It involves the members in meeting the total needs of persons. It involves the membership in fellowship activities within the context of the church. It is well organized, and it is viewed as a high priority in the life of this extremely effective church. It is a manifestation of the saying: "If you have the faith, God has the power."

6

New Mount Calvary Baptist church Los Angeles, California
Rev. Lonnie Dawson, Pastor

El Segundo and Avalon

On August 11, 1965, large segments of this community were ablaze with the conflagration of the Watts riot. A young black man had been stopped for running a red light, and an urban riot erupted in the wake of this unfortunate incident.

A few blocks away from the site of this vivid part of Los Angeles history is situated the New Mount Calvary Baptist Church. It is a church which has experienced amazing growth in the few years of its existence. It has a super Sunday School with an enrollment of more than one thousand!

The community around New Mount Calvary is a prime example of urban life in one of America's largest cities. The low- to lower middle-class neighborhood is a reflection of the complexities that come together to make up urbanity on America's contemporary scene. The ethnic composition of the neighborhood is approximately 65 percent Black and 35 percent Hispanic. This area is a post-transition area so typical of the change in ethnic composition when the neighborhood experiences transition. It is growing economically, and commercial interests proliferate, especially at the corner of El Segundo and Avalon Boulevard.

A shopping center with a multiplicity of stores makes urban shopping a convenience so familiar with modern Americans. It is an area composed of many churches. Although there is a proliferation of houses of God, there still is a gigantic spiritual need in the community. Here is a neighborhood that is blessed with stability. Most families have been there at least three or four years, and the turnover rate now is minimal. Young adults inhabit many of the homes and provide a consistency that brings an image of sameness to the community. This is an area that endures the privacy of a megalopolis in that neighbors rarely know each other and seldom become involved in one another's business. It is an area where the church plays an extremely important role and where Christianity is expected to be acted out during the week, as well as on Sunday mornings.

Roots of New Mount Calvary

What are the roots of New Mount Calvary? How did it develop into a church with a super Sunday School? The story goes back to the year 1963.

That year a young minister by the name of Lonnie Dawson felt moved that the Lord was leading him to organize a church in the area. This preacher, full of enthusiasm and ability, began to seek the Lord's will about building a church for the Lord. When the idea finally came to fruition, five persons met in the living room of the pastor's home for six months in order to start the church.

Something interesting happened on the first Sunday of the new church. When the first five people came, the pastor's heart was full of excitement at the blessings of the Lord in giving him five persons to pastor!

However, the next Sunday no one showed up. When this unusual occurrence transpired, the pastor was filled with puzzlement. He began to wonder about whether or not the Lord had really called him to start this church. His faith was severely tested by the question of: "If God has called me to start a church, then where are the people?" He began to wonder whether his dream had been visionary. After a season of prayer that day in the absence of his members, Rev. Dawson felt the assurance of the Lord: "I am with you." As a result of receiving this new assurance, Rev. Dawson went out back and built a pulpit as a symbol of his faith that the Lord was going to send somebody for him to pastor.

He then went out and talked to those members, and they began to come and bring other persons. They met in his home for six months, and during that time were able to amass savings of $512. After six months Dawson felt that the Lord had led him to a certain corner in Los Angeles where he would build a church. It was as though the Lord instructed him, "Upon this corner you will build my church." In order to acquire the house that was occupying that location, the young struggling church needed $500 which was almost exactly the amount they had saved. They moved into this house and began a building program. Today the church sits on that corner and owns property all around that particular house, and has expanded from the house to a beautiful sanctuary and educational facility which houses a membership of approximately 2,800 on roll!

In a day when many churches are succumbing to the dynamics of transition, New Mount Calvary in Los Angeles stands as a monument of successful church growth. It is one of the most dynamic churches in the Los Angeles area, and its growth statistics are impressive. Lonnie Dawson is the only pastor in the history of the church. He is a man with a brilliant mind, who has keen insights into church growth.

He has articulated the philosophy of the church as it relates to its five-point-priority emphasis plan. According to Pastor Dawson, his church has the following five major emphases:

1. To develop a strong Bible study program;
2. To develop a strong inspirational worship service;
3. To develop a close, heartfelt fellowship experience;
4. To develop a strong financial stewardship program;
5. To develop a mature mission-minded church.

This congregation appears to be well on its way into accomplishing those emphases as priorities in its life.

The New Mount Calvary Baptist Church has a large, growing membership. There are between 1,500 and 1,800 active members in a total membership of approximately 2,-800. In order to accommodate the swelling crowds on Sunday mornings, two worship services are held. A children's church accommodates the children. The church is evangelistic and averages baptizing approximately 100 persons per year. This church is not merely salvationistic. It believes in ministering to the complete needs of the whole person. As a reflection of that philosophy and commitment, the church is involved in several Christian social ministries programs. Some of those programs include: A day-care ministry during the week, an elementary school program, a reading program that involves approximately 100 young people during the summer in connection with the Seven Hundred Club, a clothes-distribution ministry where clothes are given to the needy by the tons, a free-food distribution ministry, and a radio broadcast over KTYM called the "Hour of Hope."

The New Mount Calvary Baptist Church is a member of two Baptist conventions: the Southern Baptist Convention and the National Baptist Convention of America. It participates in both conventions' programs and projects.

The Founder

Dr. Dawson is well respected by the community and the congregation, is full of enthusiasm and energy, and carries himself with quiet respectfulness. He is known to be a preacher every day of the week. His gifts in the ministry make him one of the most effective pastors in the city.

The membership of New Mount Calvary thinks highly of their pastor. They respect him as a man of God. Several terms come to mind when the congregation thinks of the pastor. First, he is a man who loves the Lord. His love for his Savior appears total and complete. Second, he is committed to his ministry. He loves his ministry and his work. He dedicates himself wholeheartedly to performing the assignment the Lord has given him. Third, he is faithful to do God's will. He simply needs to know only what God would have him do before he does it. He is the kind of man who appears to be trustworthy for divine assignments. Further, he is serious about being obedient to his Lord.

Fourth, he loves the people, caring about his congregation and the community. People find it easy to approach him in times of trouble. He does much counseling. His warm personality conveys the message that he cares about his flock.

Fifth, he has versatile skills, with many outstanding leadership abilities. He does a variety of pastoral tasks of quite well. The members are often amazed at the variety of gifts he has to invest in the task of being their leader. Sixth, he is appreciated for his administrative and organizational abilities. This pastor has had to build every program his church enjoys. His God-given abilities have served him and the congregation well in time of need. He can dream and then make that dream become reality.

Pastor Dawson, 52, is a native of Goldsboro, North Carolina. The second of five children, he graduated from high school in Goldsboro and spent four years in the military before moving to Los Angeles to take advantage of the GI Bill. He and his wife, Mamie, arrived in Los Angeles and started their lives anew. He enrolled in Compton College to begin a major in engineering. He attended Grace Bible Institute, Reed Christian College, and many seminary extension classes sponsored through the Longbeach Harbor Southern Baptist Association.

He describes himself as largely self-taught and largely self-made. He says, "I have many books by the great minds, and I read them. I study. If I could accumulate all of the training I've had, I'd have what I need." This brilliant man is a gifted leader. His leadership skills and high intelligence have earned him the position of serving as dean of the Sunday School and Baptist Training Union Congress for the Pacific District Baptist Association. In Southern Baptist Convention work, he is the former Brotherhood director and evangelism director for the Long Beach Harbor Southern Baptist Association.

Pastor Dawson is known as an able pulpiteer who can stir an audience with his fiery preaching. He is reminiscent of the traditional black Baptist pulpiteer from down South. He can attract large crowds with his rhythmic style; his musical abilities complement his preaching effectiveness.

The Super Sunday School

The Sunday School program at New Mount Calvary Baptist Church has not always been "super." There was a time when the church had approximately 500 members when only around fifty people were enrolled in Sunday School. While the church was organized with traditional programs in most areas, it did not have an effective Sunday School. The pastor felt burdened that the Lord had more for his church to do in the area of Bible study than they were doing. He began to make this a matter of prayer. He asked how the Lord would have him improve their Bible study ministry.

One night Pastor Dawson attended a Southern Baptist meeting in his association called "M Night." A speaker was Dr. J. Thurman George, the pastor of the Foxworthy Baptist Church in San Jose, California. Dr. George gave a testimony about the effectiveness of his Sunday School program and explained how his church managed to attract 1,800 persons. Pastor Dawson was fascinated by this testimony. In fact, he was astounded. There was a deep, abiding conviction that the Lord had answered his prayers about the direction which his church should take. The light had suddenly come on! Building the Sunday School was that direction. He went back to his church and began to implement the Southern Baptist Sunday School program.

As a result, his enrollment began to swell, and his church membership began to explode. He was so impacted by the miraculous turnaround of his Sunday School that he gave this testimony: "A few years ago my Sunday School enrollment was approximately fifty. Then the Lord gave me a vision of the possibilities through the Southern Baptist Sunday School approach. I trained my people in this program. Today our Sunday School enrollment is more than one thousand! Our membership is almost three thousand. Our goal is to have two thousand in Sunday School by 1990."

What are some of the ingredients necessary for a growing, dynamic Sunday School today? From the standpoint of this pastor who is doing it, the following are listed:

The pastor's commitment makes the difference. Without the involvement of the pastor, the Sunday School will have minimal growth. Without his physical presence and involvement, it is almost impossible to build a super Sunday School. Pastor Dawson is vitally involved in the Sunday

School program of his church. In fact, he is the general of the Sunday School army.

Generate enthusiasm for Sunday School evangelism at the grass-roots level. The Sunday School program should be fervently evangelistic. The laypersons need to be trained soul-winners for the Sunday School to reach people for new life in Christ. This church stresses evangelism on the part of laypersons through the Sunday School, and many people are won to Christ through the program. A Sunday School that does not major on evangelism will be powerless.

Trained leaders will make or break a Sunday School. The training of persons who lead the Sunday School ministry is extremely important. The church needs to enlist its people in qualitative training programs. The workers need to be well read in their fields of work. Pastor Dawson says, "We've read almost every book that offers approaches for growing a Sunday School." This Sunday School stresses the fact that the workers need to have tremendous expertise in order to make the Sunday School challenging for adults.

New Mount Calvary uses the Southern Baptist Sunday School program. This church stresses the principles and methodology recommended to enable churches to grow. The testimony of the pastor about the program used for Sunday School is this: "I have found that there is a language, approach, and ideology consistent throughout the Southern Baptist Sunday School work. It keeps us in the center of the road if we simply focus on that approach. It is my opinion that Southern Baptists have developed some thinking in almost every facet of Sunday School work and probably have employed some of the best men to present their points of view on what can happen to make a Sunday School grow."

A good visitation program is a must. The visitation program at New Mount Calvary extends outreach into the community. The program consists of a bus ministry and telephone visitation. Every week people go out and visit for the Sunday School. In the bus ministry, surveys are made of neighborhoods in a systematic, strategic way. Pickup is made available by three buses and one van. Each week members of the classes in the Sunday School are encouraged to make telephone contacts as a way of visiting. This has proven to be very effective in an urban area where there is often a climate of apprehension about people knocking on doors.

Weekly Workers' Meetings are extremely important. The Sunday School workers at New Mount Calvary are expected to attend Weekly Workers' Meetings. This gives them an opportunity to revive their energies for Sunday School work and an opportunity to learn more about the Sunday School program. It makes it possible for the sharing of information and the coordination of planning for an effective Sunday School.

Use topflight literature in your Sunday School. New Mount Calvary uses Southern Baptist literature. The pastor says, "I find it most effective for several reasons. First of all, where the ideas come from is not the major emphasis. We do it because it's a good idea, a good thought, a good process. The principles don't have color. Methods don't have color." This Sunday School uses the wide variety of literature and resources available through its denomination.

Focus priority attention on reaching adults for Sunday School involvement. New Mount Calvary has majored on reaching adults for the Sunday School. In a day when many still believe that Sunday School is for children only, this church proves that many adults will be responsive to an adequate challenge for Sunday School.

Keep a good prospect file. This Sunday School has an up-to-date prospect file on many people who could become involved in the Sunday School program at the church. They have a system for getting the names of new prospects on an ongoing basis. As a result of having this prospect file, potential new members are easily identified and enlisted for Sunday School participation.

Make sure that you provide enough space for good, quality teaching. Certain teacher-class ratios should be maintained, and an adequate teaching space should be allocated for each class. The church recently completed the construction of a new educational building that helps house some twenty-seven classes of Sunday School activity. The pastor believes it is important for the church to provide adequate space for the teaching activity.

The Sunday School program at New Mount Calvary Baptist Church is one of the strongest in California. It is a super story!

7

Greenforest Baptist Church
Decatur, Georgia
Dr. George McCalep, Pastor

Context

The birth pains of the civil rights movement have delivered a new community in South DeKalb County, Georgia. The trauma of a decade ago in the area of human rights had a strong impact on this Atlanta suburb. South Dekalb County was considered a hot seat during the civil rights movement. During this upheaval of social change, it was one of the leading centers of controversy. However, due to the persistent winds of history, this area is now racially mixed.

The visitor is greeted by a neat neighborhood of homes valued in excess of $50,000 each. It is clearly a middle-class community composed of homeowners. This suburban area has gone through a racial transition. It is now approximately 80 percent black and 20 percent white. Signs of growth abound within the context of the community.

At 2135 Shamrock Drive is a church building which is unusual. This is the Greenforest Baptist Church, an anachronism in the minds of many people, a church predominantly black today (but was organized as a Southern Baptist church with a white membership more than twenty-five years ago). It has an enrollment of approximately three-fourths of its membership in Sunday School!

The Greenforest Baptist Church, still Southern Baptist,

has a tremendous Sunday School program. How does a church in the black community manage to enroll three-fourths of its members in Sunday School when the typical black church probably has no more than 15 percent? What kind of church can have such a success?

The Koinonia

The history of the Greenforest Baptist Church goes back to the 1950s when it was organized as a Southern Baptist congregation, dedicated to reaching its community which was white at the time. Under the ministry of several pastors the membership of the congregation grew to approximately seven hundred before falling victim to the classic transitional syndrome. As the neighborhood changed, the church fell upon hard times but exhibited a determination to minister to the changing community. However, due to an inability to attract a sufficient number of people from the community during the days of transition, the church experienced a falling away, and its membership dwindled to about one hundred before a crisis in its life developed.

In 1978 an exodus of the pastor and most of the white members 'occurred. On one Sunday morning, apparently without much warning, the black members arrived at church to discover that the white pastor and the members had moved their membership away. This was a painful experience for the approximately twenty-five black members who remained. They had come with a dream of fulfilling the ideal of multiracial Christian brotherhood within a congregational context, only to face the stark reality that, for the present, it was not going to be their experience.

The Atlanta Baptist Association assisted the new black church during its formative years. Rev. John Cross, a black staff member from the Atlanta Baptist Association (and a

well-respected leader in interracial ministry), was called to
be interim pastor of the church for approximately one year.
He assisted the congregation in recouping. The association
offered financial assistance to help the church deal with its
difficult crisis. In August, 1979, the church called its first
black pastor in the person of Dr. George McCalep, a college
professor, and began to experience a rapid growth. Since the
coming of Dr. McCalep as pastor, the church has grown at
the rate of almost two hundred members per year.

The Greenforest Church of today is an interesting congregation. It is highly diversified in its membership, having
attracted people from various Baptist traditions, as well as
those from Methodist, Presbyterian, Catholic, and Pen-
tecostal traditions. Educationally, the church membership is
composed mostly of high achievers. Approximately 75 percent of the adults are college graduates. This is a young
congregation with the average age of its membership being
about thirty-seven years old. It is a family-oriented church
with a goodly number of children. It has a large number of
formerly married persons within its membership. The
church is made up of persons who have been called "recap-
tured church folks," persons who have been turned off by
religion in the past or who have experienced pain and have
now found a meaningful involvement in a caring church
which meets their needs.

This suburban church is involved in a wide variety of
ministries to the people of the church and community.
Among the social ministries of the church are the following:
a benevolence ministry for people in times of crisis, a food
pantry, a clothes closet, participation in "meals on wheels,"
a deaf ministry, a singles ministry, workshops on teenage
pregnancy, career-day emphases, aerobic classes, a nurses'
guild, and sponsorship of the Boy Scouts, Girl Scouts, and
Cub Scouts. The ministries of the church have attracted

community attention. In fact, the county gave the church a grant of $10,000 to set up another crisis ministry similar to the one at the church. The church believes that at least 10 percent of its budget should go to the area of ministering to the social needs of persons.

The Greenforest Church now has a membership of around 800. It is known for four primary emphases. It majors on Bible teaching. It is well organized. It reaches out into the community to help others, constantly starting new ministries. For a new church, six years old, it has experienced unusual growth and has been able to reach unusual heights in effectiveness.

When a person travels down Shamrock Avenue, he will encounter a large church building with contemporary architecture. The nontraditional architecture is a hint that herein thrives a congregation that is atypical and nontraditional. The pastor is well educated. The church is time conscious. The worship services are nonemotional. The membership comes from various backgrounds. The Sunday School has almost six hundred persons enrolled. The Greenforest Baptist Church is symbolic of the new wave of churches within the black community dedicated to a holistic ministry, coupled with first-rate programming and leadership.

Solomon

Greenforest has the privilege of being led by one of the best-educated pastors within the Southern Baptist Convention. Dr. George McCalep was reared in Normal, Alabama, on the campus of Alabama A & M University where his father served as a college professor in various capacities for forty-four years. Dr. McCalep graduated from Alabama A & M University where he received his bachelor of science degree in 1960. He graduated from the University of Kansas in 1964 with a master of science degree. He received his master's certification from the John Carroll University in 1976. In 1977, he graduated with his doctor of philosophy from Ohio State University with a major in physical education and sociology. In 1980, he earned his master of divinity degree from the Interdenominational Theological Center, Morehouse School of Religion.

In college he was an outstanding athlete in football, baseball, basketball, and tennis. In fact, he was the captain of the football team and the tennis team. He later served as a coach in football, basketball, and track. The forty-six-year-old pastor still looks like he could hold his own on an athletic field.

He has been employed as a teacher in public and private schools; has also been a sales executive with Waddell and Reed in Cleveland, Ohio; has served as owner/manager of National Financial Services. He is presently a professor at the Georgia State University. From 1961 through 1973 he was a "registered broker and principal" with the National Association of Security Dealers.

He is active in the Atlanta Baptist Association, affiliated with the Southern Baptist Convention, and serves on the executive board. He is also a member of the committee which deals with churches in transition. He is also active with the Southeastern Committee on Physical Education for the YMCA.

He and his wife, Sadie, have three children: Michael, George, and Timothy.

Dr. McCalep is a combination of many interesting characteristics. This tall, athletic Georgian stands like a Samson ready to slay the enemies of the Lord. The combination of a brilliant mind and a forceful personality collaborate to make him a formidable leader. When the members of Greenforest look at the man in the pulpit, they are impressed by God's generosity in "gifting" individuals. Clearly, this is one of God's strong men.

Those who encounter George McCalep are introduced to a man with a dynamic personality. He is alive! He is on fire! He is energetic! His personality symbolizes the activity of God in the human experience.

He is viewed as an outstanding teacher, obviously blessed in this area through the possession of a brilliant intellect and outstanding teaching gifts. He is able to translate his talents into an impactful teaching tool. Listeners who attend his church feast on divine wisdom from on high from the lips of this gifted pedagogue. Those who sit under the ministry of George McCalep are soon convinced that he is a shepherd who can feed the flock.

As a pulpiteer, Pastor McCalep is known as an able preacher. His sermon content is informative and creates a sense of excitement among the listeners. It makes it easy for him to hold the attention of the audience as he expounds theology from the Lord. He is not long-winded and knows when to end a sermon. His preaching style is "nonperformance oriented." He is not a "whooper," not an emotionalizer of the audience, although he believes in the normal flow of emotions. He does not "put on a show" in the pulpit. In fact, his sermons are characterized by a powerful dignity flowing from his well-cultured mind.

Dr. McCalep's leadership style is built around the foundation of punctuality. Meetings start on time and end on time. Presentations are geared to the attention span of the listeners. Time is a valued commodity in his ministry and is not wasted.

This bivocational college professor/pastor is known for his open-mindedness. He does not have a closed approach to information; he is always open to the possibility of growing. Not all of the questions have been answered in his philosophy. He is a person who suspends judgment on issues and situations until he has the opportunity to develop sufficient information on the subject.

Pastor McCalep is concerned about the community and is known as a conscientious worker who spends long hours involved in meeting the needs of people. He is also available for pastoral counseling and counsels many. There is a down-to-earth dimension about his personality that says: "This pastor cares enough to be involved with the hurts of ordinary people. Though he is well educated, he is not a snob and always manages to find time for ministry to hurting humanity.

Dr. McCalep is also characterized by the virtue of patience. When many other people's patience has long ago run out, his still remains. He manages to maintain his composure and remain calm in the midst of trying situations. He will go the second and third miles, if necessary, for the sake of the Kingdom.

Sunday School at Greenforest

The Sunday School hour at Greenforest is full of activity. Excitement is written all over the faces of boys and girls, as well as adults, as they enter the church to participate in its Sunday School. Sunday morning at Greenforest is not ordinary as it relates to its religious education ministry. It is extraordinary. This Sunday School utilizes a growth-oriented Sunday School approach. It utilizes the Sunday School program of the Southern Baptist Sunday School Board. The program is characterized by an emphasis on reaching people through the Sunday School. The well-trained staff operates this highly organized Sunday School program with the efficiency of a machine for Sunday School growth. Age-level methodology is on target as it is used to motivate and teach the students. There is an ever-present emphasis on always being on the lookout to contact persons for Sunday School through a program of "constant contact consciousness."

How does this Sunday School manage to involve approximately three-fourths of its membership on Sunday morning? What dynamics exist to enable this church to stand out in an age of abandonment of Sunday School emphasis in the black community?

In response to a question about the analysis of his Sunday School's success, Dr. McCalep suggests the following as ingredients for growing a dynamic Sunday School:

A desire on the part of the pastor to see the Sunday School grow is essential. The pastor must have a value system and philosophy which emphasizes the Sunday School. If he does not have it, it will not grow. The pastor is the key leader at the church, and if he is not ready to lead the congregation into building a dynamic Sunday School, then the mini-Sunday School will be the result.

There must be a commitment on the part of the pastor and the church to reach people through the Sunday School. This must be a priority if it is to be successful. The church and the pastor need to be committed.

The church must have an effective organizational plan for Sunday School growth. Without a plan, the commitment cannot be implemented. The church must have an effective plan to reach people through the Sunday School. In the case of Greenforest the effective organizational plan is the Southern Baptist Sunday School program, a program even used by eleven or twelve other denominations. There is a certain philosophy and set of principles used by this church which yield the conclusion: it is possible to grow a Sunday School.

Well-trained and committed teachers are essential for building a growing Sunday School. If the teaching quality is inferior, the attendance quality will also be inferior. The latest teaching methodology is made available to them, and contemporary ideas on relating to people in a learning setting are shared with them. They participate in study courses and earn awards in the various areas of Sunday School work as an avenue of keeping abreast of what is going on in the field.

The Sunday School should be viewed as a place through which ministry occurs, in addition to the teaching of the Word. The concept of shared ministry is implemented through the Sunday School in this church. A Sunday School class, for example, is not simply the place where the Bible is taught. It is a place where ministry needs of the members are met. It is a venture of caring about the members.

The church must actually implement the plan. The organizational plan will not be effective unless it is actually implemented. Nothing replaces the implementation of the plan. If it is not implemented, the Sunday School will not grow.

There should be a commitment to small-class utilization. There is an optimum size for each Sunday School class, and it should be maintained. Large classes are usually counterproductive, although there are some outstanding exceptions. The idea of the small class promotes the idea of intimacy needed for personalized ministry among the members.

Enlist and use talented persons in leadership, regardless of gender. There should be no place for sexism in growing a dynamic Sunday School. In fact, the director of the Sunday School at Greenforest is a committed woman who is an astute leader in Sunday School work. In some Sunday Schools, traditional offices have been reserved for men. This pastor believes that the church should not be chauvinistic in the utilization of persons in leadership.

The church should provide adequate space for implementing a worthy teaching experience. Greenforest has at least thirty-four classrooms, and they are used in the Sunday School program. The Sunday School is given space priority within the church.

Practice evangelism through the Sunday School. The Sunday School is a place that ought to be concerned about the relationship of people to Jesus Christ. In Greenforest, approximately 30 percent of the baptisms come through the Sunday School. An evangelistic invitation is given once a month in the Sunday School with great effectiveness. This Sunday School cares about the spiritual life of persons and it makes a great effort to lead every person to the Lord Jesus Christ.

Start new units often. New units tend to grow faster than old units. Therefore, it is easier to reach more people with the new units. When a class reaches its optimum size, another should be started.

Remember to utilize the basics of Sunday School growth. There are several principles that have been demonstrated successfully down through the years in churches with growing Sunday Schools. These are the basics of Sunday School growth. They should be utilized because they work in a black context.

• Observe the Sunday School Standard as a goal for your Sunday School. The Sunday School Standard is a system that suggests goals for a growing Sunday School. If a church achieves these goals, it will grow, according to history. A church can have a concrete measuring rod against which to measure its progress and needs by utilizing the Sunday School Standard.

• Focus on adults. It should not be assumed that Sunday School is for children only. There are many adults who are potentially great prospects for involvement in Sunday School work under the proper conditions. They should be challenged to become involved in Sunday School. At Greenforest, adults make up approximately 40 percent of those involved.

• Remember the importance of the Weekly Workers' Meeting. The Weekly Workers' Meeting is extremely important for the growth of the Sunday School. It is so pivotal that a church probably will not grow through the Sunday School without a meaningful Weekly Workers' Meeting. There is good literature available on how to conduct a meaningful meeting. This church has discovered that a Weekly Workers' Meeting can be a tremendous shot in the arm for growing a Sunday School.

Greenforest is experiencing a renaissance. At such a young age in its rebirth, it already has become extremely effective. By comparison with most churches on a percentage basis, its Sunday School is simply outstanding. It is a church we will hear from in the future.

8

New Way
Fellowship Baptist Church
Miami, Florida
Rev. Billy Baskin, Pastor

The Neighborhood

The friendly sun beams down on this South Florida city. The gentle breeze provides natural air conditioning for this vacation resort. The mild, humid climate beckons for senior citizens in the sunset of their days. The azure skies enframe a community that has recently been embroiled in controversy. The dynamics of future shock have rocked this community in the past few years. Migration, displacement, transition, and a socially volatile climate have conspired to give Miami, Florida, headlines full of drama during the last five years. Within this context stands the New Way Fellowship Baptist Church.

The New Way Fellowship Baptist Church is located in the Carol City-Opa Locka area. It is a community of approximately 15,000 people caught up in the urban hubbub of transition. The neighborhood is mixed and changing; its residents are approximately 65 percent black, 10 percent white, and 25 percent Hispanic.

The neighborhood is made up primarily of single-family dwellings interspersed with a few apartments. Most of the people would probably be classified as semiprofessionals with lower to middle incomes. The Florida Memorial College and the Saint Thomas Villanova College are nearby.

The neighborhood is approximately twenty miles from the resort area of Miami Beach and seven miles from the urban area of Liberty City, recently racked by urban rioting. The city of Miami has an Hispanic mayor and a Black police chief. The Cuban/Black political coalition is potent in the area. Amid this urban context is the New Way Fellowship Baptist Church, one of the fastest-growing churches in America with one of the largest Sunday Schools in the black community.

The Church

The New Way Fellowship Baptist Church is one of the strong churches in America today. It has the distinction of having grown to a membership of over 3,000 in only ten years of existence. During this time its Sunday School has grown to a gargantuan 1,100-plus enrollment. How does this church manage to enroll so many people in Sunday School? What kind of church is able to perform this unusual feat?

New Way Fellowship has a short history. It goes back to 1975 when the Rev. Billy Baskin was led to organize a new church in Miami. After an unfulfilling prior pastorate in the city, Rev. Baskin resigned, and 125 persons met with him to organize a new church. It was the desire of the new group to organize a New Testament church which would be biblically based and totally serious about being on mission for the Lord. The new congregation wished to remain a viable black church while being open to everybody. This church was committed to the concept of building and equipping people for the work of the Lord. This congregation chose the name "New Way" because it wanted to do the Lord's work in a new way that was not encumbered by the traditions of the past.

In 1976 the church purchased its first building and began

to experience brisk growth. During the next decade the membership would grow to more than 3,100, and they would baptize an average of 150 people per year. The Sunday School enrollment would exceed 1,100. In a stable church community saturated with approximately fifteen churches within a two-mile radius, New Way Fellowship has enjoyed an exciting ministry. It became a church with an orientation toward family ministry. It has demonstrated flexibility in worship while maintaining a spontaneity and sense of liveliness that has excited the worshipers. It is a functional church with effective worship, punctuated with a variety of music. It has progressive programming that far outdistances the traditional emphasis of many black churches. It has a far-reaching missions program, a farflung outreach program, and an effective Christian education program. It endeavors to meet the needs of the community. Under the able leadership of Pastor Baskin this new congregation has discovered a pragmatic new way to be on mission for the Lord.

While it emphasizes evangelism it also concentrates on social concerns. It has a balanced ministry; it does not believe that the ministry of the church should be dichotomized. It believes that a healthy church will be involved in total ministry. As a result of this philosophy of wholeness, the congregation is involved in several social ministries: a jail and prison ministry for those incarcerated in the area, a ministry to troubled teens who may be undergoing serious problems, a ministry to unwed mothers in the area, a weekly food distribution ministry, a tutorial program for those with academic difficulty, and a drug counseling ministry for those in danger of chemical abuse. It is supportive of the National Association for the Advancement of Colored People. It addresses the needs of the community in the area of crime, unemployment, and displaced families. It cares about the community in which it is located.

The New Way Fellowship Baptist Church is a dually-aligned with the Southern Baptist Convention and the National Baptist Convention, USA, Incorporated. It is a leading church, in many respects, in both Conventions.

The Founder-Pastor

Rev. Billy Baskin is an imposing physical specimen of a preacher. He stands over six-feet tall and carries a professional lineman's weight on a compact muscular frame. He has the quiet dignity of a Samson stamped upon his face. He has a no-nonsense manner that symbolizes total commitment to doing the work of the Lord. Slightly balding, he has the distinguished look of a scholar. He is an immaculate dresser whose appearance inspires pride on the part of the congregation when they lay eyes upon him. He is a symbol of the new breed of pastor in urban black America: youthful, intelligent, articulate, progressive, and able. He is a big man physically and spiritually.

This mild-mannered pastor is a native of Florida. He was born in Perry, Florida, in 1938 in the home of a pastor, Rev. Charles Baskin. He graduated from high school in Perry and enrolled in the United States Army. He graduated from Florida Memorial College with a bachelor of science degree and the Florida Atlantic College with a master of arts degree. He has continued studies at the Interdenominational Theological Center and the New York Theological Seminary. New Way Fellowship is his third pastorate. Prior to organizing this church he pastored the New Macedonia Baptist Church in Tampa, Florida, and the First Baptist Church at Bunch Park, Florida.

In denominational circles he is viewed as a capable leader.

Other ministers tend to gravitate to him. His leadership ability has been recognized by his peers, and he has been elected president of the ministers and deacons organization for the Florida East Coast Association. He has also been selected Bible teacher for the General Baptist State Convention of Florida's Women's Division. He is the chairman of the evangelism committee for the Miami Baptist Association. He is a man whose leadership ability is greatly respected.

Pastor Baskin is married to the former Katherine Patterson. They have four children: Wendell, Jeffery, Cynthia, and Ayanna.

Pastor Baskin is perceived by his members to have many outstanding characteristics. He is a good listener, one who knows how to be still and hear the other person's point of view. He has the patience to be the recipient of information from a burdened parishioner. Because of his listening ability, people find it easy to approach him concerning their problems.

He is a powerful preacher. He has been used as keynote speaker across the country in national meetings in the Southern Baptist Convention and in the National Baptist Convention. He is an articulate orator who has a formidable presence in the pulpit. A master communicator, he knows how to hold the attention of the audience. He is humorous and can move an audience to applaud the profundity of his message. He knows how to put words together like a wordsmith in order to have the optimum impact upon an audience. He has a warm sermonic style that puts the audience at ease. His logic is compelling and persuasive as he drives home his point. His preaching style is ease to listen to; his keen intellect is manifested in his sermonizing and enables him to feed the people who are hungry for the Word of God. Sunday morning at 11 during the worship service is a thrilling event at the New Way Fellowship Baptist Church when Pastor Baskin is in the pulpit. It is a time of celebration without empty emotionalism. It is a time of rich joy in the Lord based on feasting from God's Word. The delivery he employs has a mixture of the traditional black-preaching style with the best of modern oratory. This preacher can paint the picture with his artistic vocabulary.

His members view him as being an effective teacher. His brilliant mind, combined with a consecrated spirit, enables him to dig deep into the Word of God and share with his parishioners. He is attuned to contemporary trends in education; he understands the dynamics of good teaching and utilizes this understanding in his delivery. He is well prepared and knowledgeable on a broad range of subjects. He believes in trying to keep up with the contemporary scene, so he can be relevant as he feeds his flock.

Pastor Baskin is a personable minister. He has a warm, friendly smile for everyone he encounters. He has a lively sense of humor often sprinkled through his conversation. People feel comfortable around him. He conveys the impression that he likes the people—as well as loves them. He is the prototypical, nice-guy pastor.

He is open to new ideas. Part of his personality includes a willingness to consider that which is nontraditional. His personality seems to be identified by an openness to a *new way* of doing things, and his creativity quotient is high. He is interested in seeing what might work, and he is not afraid of a challenge and not intimidated by the alibi, "We've never done it that way before." He is willing to consider every legitimate possibility.

Baskin is totally committed to the Lord, serious about his Christianity and practicing his religion. His Christian faith is contagious and inspires devotion on the part of those who are close to him.

Baskin is a builder, a builder of people through the instru-
mentality of religious education, a builder of buildings for
the glory of God. His most significant accomplishment, he
feels, has been in the area of building a vital Bible teaching
program and building a house of worship for the Lord. The
effectiveness of his people-building emphasis is seen in the
tremendous response of his people to Sunday School. The
effectiveness of his building may be seen in the erection of
a magnificent worship center made of split-face marble with
a modern architectural design symbolic of an ark. It houses
a worship center on the second floor and an educational
facility on the first floor. The educational facility houses
forty-six classes and has twenty-four convertible classrooms.

Under the leadership of Pastor Baskin, New Way Fellowship has become a most attractive church in the community.
The building dominates the area at 16800 Northwest 22nd
Avenue. The lovely sanctuary contributes to the atmosphere
of worship each Sunday morning. The pastor's study with
its modern design gives the impression that it is a place of
light from on high. The modern elevator carrying members
from the first to the second floor lends an atmosphere of
modernity to this up-to-date church.

The members of New Way Fellowship are impressed with
their membership. The church is viewed as being unique
among churches in the area because of its progressive programming. It is an exciting place to be on Sunday morning.
The visitor can feel the sense of electricity permeating the
congregation as they prepare for worship. They feel that
their church is on the cutting edge of a progressive movement for the Lord. It is a Spirit-filled church where the Holy
Spirit is in control, a biblically-oriented church that believes
in studying the Word of God, so people may develop into
the kind of persons the Lord would have them become.

The New Way Sunday School

The Sunday School program at New Way is one of the most exciting in the nation. In a relatively short time, this church has managed to grow a large Sunday School. It has forty-six classes, fifty-eight workers, and more than 1,100 enrolled in Sunday School! It uses the Southern Baptist Sunday School program and literature.

What would this gifted pastor of this super Sunday School recommend to churches interested in growing a dynamic Sunday School? According to Pastor Baskin, several suggestions may be helpful in growing a dynamic Sunday School.

Commitment on the part of the pastor is essential. The pastor is the leading motivator in the church. If he is not committed to Sunday School, the church will not take it seriously. He must be a Sunday School pastor. If he expects his church to make Sunday School an important part of the agenda, he must personally make it one of his priorities.

The church needs a conscious commitment to growth through the Sunday School. Without the involvement and commitment of the church, the Sunday School will not grow. One of the key skills needed by the pastor of the church with a growing Sunday School is the ability to persuade the church to be committed to growing through the Sunday School.

Committed teachers are an invaluable asset to the growing Sunday School. Teachers should have a life-style consistent with the gospel of Jesus Christ. They need to be consecrated Christians who love the Lord, who will pay the price to become excellent Sunday School workers. They must accept the fact that they are called to expand their horizons and broaden their skills so they may have maximum effectiveness in the classroom.

There should be an adequate number of teachers for the size of the class.

Proper teacher/student ratios should be maintained. There are excellent guides that recommend proper teacher/student ratios. The Sunday School should do everything within its power to maintain a good, balanced relationship between the number of students and the number of teachers.

The Sunday School should keep up with and use first-rate resources for Sunday School. Not every Sunday School program is alike. A growth-oriented Sunday School produces growth. The Sunday School should be aware of this program and implement it in its ministry. There are outstanding materials and literature available, written to meet the needs of particular categories of people. In addition to first-rate quarterlies, there are resource kits, teaching-picture sets, videotaped resources, resources in braille, resources in other languages, and a host of other Sunday School helps to assist a Sunday School in being a maximum experience. The Sunday School does not have to be limited merely to the availability of teacher's quarterlies and pupil's quarterlies. There are many resources that can help a Sunday School grow in its community.

There should be an outreach emphasis in the Sunday School. Visitation is a must for a growing Sunday School. The church cannot passively sit back and expect people to take the initiative to come and join it. The church must go after them wherever they are. The church that cares enough to go after people succeeds in having them come. The Sunday School visitation program is a powerful part of reaching people for the gospel and the church.

Pastor Baskin has tried it and succeeded. His experience proves that many people in the community can be reached through the Sunday School. His word to pastors who would like to know how to do it is simply this: "Get involved. Recognize the potential. The Sunday School is the strongest organization we have for reaching people."

9

The Cathedral of Faith Inkster, Michigan
Dr. J. Herbert Hinkle, Pastor

Quotations in many places are from Dr. Hinkle's book, *How to Reach Multitudes for Christ* (Grand Rapids, MI: New Hope Press, 1979).

A Different Stroke

As the visitor walks into the vestibule, he/she is greeted by a prominent sign that reads, "No smoking! No drinking! No obscenity! No vulgarity! No profanity! here in the cathedral. Women are not to wear pants in worship. Men are never welcome with their hair in corn rows. Men are to remove hats when entering this holy building! Be respectful and courteous. Dr. J. Herbert Hinkle, Divine Leader."

When a person enters the Cathedral of Faith in Inkster, Michigan, he is greeted by a stately looking lady with a white floor-length dress who smiles and greets you enthusiastically, "Bless you with love and peace." The ornate, gold-trimmed twin mirrors in the vestibule immediately reflect the visitors' presence on the wall. Padded, multistriped, blue-and-orange-muted doors provide a friendly invitation into the sanctuary of the church. Blue shag carpet adorns the floor, and attractive bulletin boards provide an impressive welcome as one walks through the doors. This is the building of the Cathedral of Faith. It symbolizes the idea that something unusual goes on here.

One of the unusual occurrences at the Cathedral of Faith has been its impressive Sunday School program. The Cathedral of Faith may hold the modern record for high attendance on one Sunday in any Sunday School of the black community in America. On one Sunday in 1976, it attracted 3,749 persons to its Sunday School program! In its heyday, its Sunday School attendance averaged over 900 on Sunday morning. It is now in a period of rebuilding its Sunday School after a falling away in enrollment. However, according to the pastor, it still has over 1,200 people on roll for Sunday School.

What kind of church can attract almost 4,000 persons in the black community to its Sunday School? What kind of genius does it require in order to work such a miracle?

The Cathedral of Faith is located in the Detroit suburb of Inskter, Michigan. Inkster is approximately 30,000 population with a 50-50 black-white ratio in the community. It is surrounded by predominantly white suburbs. It is a solid upper-middle-class community of affluent persons. Every third or fourth house probably has a boat or recreational vehicle. It is estimated that most of the adults in the community have attended some college. This community of middle-class homes probably has a median income in excess of $20,000. The community has well-kept neighborhoods, good schools, and an economy heavily dependent on the automobile industry. The black community is empowered in the political arena. This is demonstrated by the fact that three of the last four mayors have been blacks. A large number of the black population is made up of transplanted Southerners who migrated north to escape the ravages of Jim Crow and the segregation system in the South. These people moved up North seeking a land of opportunity and found it in the Motor City.

The Fellowship of the New Beginning

The Cathedral of Faith is an impressive complex standing on nine acres of prime property in Inkster. What are the roots of this church?

The church goes back to February 9, 1930, when the Peace and Harmony Baptist Church was organized under the tutelge of Rev. A. G. Oliver. The church originally consisted of forty-five members. Rev. Oliver had a short tenure, lasting only eleven months. He was succeeded in December, 1930, by Rev. William Wooten. Wooten served until 1932 and was succeeded by Rev. O. B. Jones in December of that year. In 1932 the church changed its name to the Second Baptist Church. Under the ministry of the Rev. Jones, a building was erected on the corner of Williams and Chestnut. Pastor Jones resigned in 1954 due to poor health, and Rev. Charles W. Poole was elected as pastor that year. Pastor Poole served until 1958 and was succeeded by Rev. S. L. Hampton as pastor of the Second Baptist Church. Pastor Hampton served until 1969 and was followed by Dr. J. Herbert Hinkle.

Under the ministry of Dr. Hinkle, the church has made lengthy strides in creative ministry to the needs of its community. It experienced a tremendous increase in membership, and especially of the Sunday School. Under the ministry of Dr. Hinkle, the name was changed to the Cathedral of Faith.

What kind of church is the Cathedral of Faith? How does it do its work?

The Cathedral of faith is known as a church with standards. It is a church where not everything goes. They believe in practicing those things that, in their opinion, glorify the name of the Lord. For example, the church has a dress code that is practically enforced. It has certain expectations for people who work in its program.

It believes in being led by God. The trends of society are not designed to lead the church, in the philosophy of this church. God alone has the right to lead the church in all of its activities.

It is a friendly church. Though its membership ranges from Ph.D.s on down, it is a church that is not cold or distant to the newcomer. Members enthusiastically participate in the worship service, get to know each other, and happily greet one another with the statement: "Bless you with love and peace."

It is an active congregation, believing in ministry in the community. Several leading officials of the community are members of the congregation, including a city councilman, the city clerk, the fire chief, and a large number of businessmen. The pastor has been a candidate for mayor.

The church loves people. The hurting people of society are expected to receive the ministry of the church. The church believes in going the extra mile in trying to help people. It believes that when people have needs, they ought to be able to come to the church, and the church should be willing to help.

The congregation loves the pastor. There is an atmosphere of respect when he walks in, a climate of warm acceptance as he preaches the Word of God. As one lady put it, when I visited the church, "Dr. Hinkle has been our pastor now for sixteen years. We sure do love him."

The Cathedral of Faith believes in the people of God praying and playing together. The church believes faith can be fun. Therefore, many creative types of activities are planned to minister to the needs of the people. For example, one of the ministries of the church was called "Old-Fashioned Sunday." The pastor encouraged the members to dress in old clothes of yesteryear. He dressed as George Washington and rode a wagon to church that day. It was a time of genuine fun.

This church emphasizes prosperity. The church believes that, as a part of its ministry, it has the responsibility of helping people learn how to handle money. The trappings of the church reflect a belief in success motivation and possibility thinking. The church endeavors to help people be able to live well in this present world.

Denominationalism is deemphasized now at the Cathedral of Faith. Although the church and the pastor come from traditional Baptist backgrounds, this does not appear to be emphasized at present. The church, however, still does maintain fellowship involvement with churches in different denominations.

Theologically, the church is fundamentalistic. It is basically theologically conservative. A statement in a brochure from the church states the doctrinal position like this: "We are a Bible-believing, sin-hating, soul-winning, tithing church!!!" The church believes in the verbal inspiration of the Scriptures, the existence of a literal hell and heaven, the virgin birth of Jesus, the sacrificial death of Jesus, the bodily resurrection of Jesus, the literal return of Jesus Christ to this earth, baptism by immersion, and being filled with the Holy Ghost.

The central thrust of the Cathedral of Faith seems to be summed up in this statement from the church: "The secret of living is fruit-bearing. God did not create you, and Christ did not die for you that you might go through life getting. God created you and Christ purchased you that you might invest your life giving. If you refuse to bear fruit, you will miss the true meaning and glory of the Christian life. If you yield to Christ and permit His life to create His fruit through you, then you will really live."

The church has a definite philosophy about the nature of the ministry God expects it to render. It has a clear blueprint in terms of where it needs to go, and it has strategies for fulfilling the demands of the blueprint. The philosophy and blueprint of the ministries of the Cathedral of Faith have been stated as follows in the book titled *How to Reach Multitudes for Christ* by Dr. J. Herbert Hinkle. In this book, the philosophy of the church is stated like this: "It is my position, however, that the church must be concerned, and must use every means available to reach every available person in every available way with the Gospel of Jesus Christ. If there is a job in the community that needs to be done in the name of the Lord Jesus Christ and for His glory, the church must be convinced of its duty to do that job.

"At the Cathedral, we feel that before us is an unlimited potential of souls in our community to be reached for Christ. God has established us (the local church) to be the means of carrying the Gospel of Jesus Christ to the whole world. We have made ourselves the launching pad of evangelism, soul-winning, disciple enlistment, and Christian training.

"We recognize the need for a Bible-centered, Christ-exalting, aggressive local church that reaches the lost for Jesus Christ. Here·is the blueprint we are using to pass the Word of the Lord out":

Soul-Winning. This church believes that the Bible truly commands each Christian to be actively involved in winning souls to the Lord. The pastor states, "We conduct a soul-winning institute each Sunday evening to train people how to witness. People cannot be overtrained in the field of soul-winning.

Taping Ministry. The worship services conducted at the Cathedral of Faith are tape recorded and made available for listeners, absentees, or shut-ins who request them.

Library and Book Store. The pastor reports that the church has a library and a book store operated daily. "I have learned that many people are not aware of the abundance of quality Christian literature available today. Since many would not drive to the nearest Christian book store, we brought the store to them," he states.

Convalescent Home Ministry. This ministry consists of a minister and deacon going every other week to convalescent homes in the area to preach and pass out tracts, handle prayer requests, and minister to the needs of convalescents.

Sunday School. Dr. Hinkle states, "Our Sunday School serves as the hotbed for evangelism. We have a departmentalized Sunday School that is set up with two purposes in mind: to evangelize our community and to indoctrinate in the teaching of Jesus Christ those souls that have been won."

Printing Ministry. The church is in the business of printing its message as well as saying it verbally. "We print thousands of pieces of literature that carry the Gospel of Jesus Christ. We use letters, postcards, newspapers, books, tracts, and sermons," according to the pastor.

Bus Ministry. The church believes in using buses to provide transportation for people, especially those who will ride to Sunday School. At one time in its history, the church had as many as fifteen buses operating on Sunday mornings to bus people to Sunday School. Although this ministry has been temporarily suspended, the church has plans to reactivate it shortly.

Bible Study Leaders. The church trains people who are not involved in bus ministry or the Sunday School to be teachers in the homes of new members. In addition to this ministry, there are two new-member classes.

Deaf Ministry. The church has a ministry to the deaf. During the worship services a dactylologist signs the language of the worship service.

Youth Ministry. The church believes in reaching young people socially and spiritually. The pastor says, "Our one major goal is to reach the youth for Jesus Christ. To help us reach this goal, we utilize the Awana Clubs, Christian Action Workers, conferences, camps, Bible class, visitation, summer recreation, and field trips."

Family Counseling. An assistant minister for the church counsels families with problems. Premarital counseling is also conducted. Occasionally, Christian psychologists are brought in to conduct seminars in family counseling for the church.

Cathedral Prayer Group. The Cathedral Prayer Group is a group of persons who pray for the ministry of the church. Dr. Hinkle says, "We believe that God honors prayer and that any ministry ought to be bathed in prayer."

Cathedral Petite Academy. This ministry consists of a day-care center where Bible stories are used to introduce children to the gospel of Jesus Christ.

Herbert Hinkle Bible Institute. The Herbert Hinkle Bible Institute is a ministry that was set in operation in order that "pastors, associate pastors, missionaries, music leaders, teachers, and secretaries may be better equipped to do the work of the Lord." "The goal of the institute is to train the student to be Spirit filled, cultured, appropriate, and able to do a first-class work for the Lord."

Mortuary. A mortuary ministry has been set up through which a trained counselor ministers to the spiritual needs of the bereaved, in addition to the traditional funeral involvement. The mortuary is located next door to the church and has been described as having "the most beautiful funeral chapel in town."

Radio Ministry. The Cathedral of Faith has three radio broadcasts per week. One is on radio station WCHB in Detroit and the other on WLAC in Nashville, Tennessee.

Television Ministry. The church has had a ministry through the medium of television where worship services were broadcast.

The Cathedral of Faith has a membership of approximately 1,200 families which make up between an estimated 2,500 to 3,000 members.

Moses

The pastor of the Cathedral of Faith is the Dr. J. Herbert Hinkle who is described in a church brochure as "a middle-aged gentleman who has been preaching since age seven." This one-time boy preacher has matured into a formidable force for the Lord in his adult years. At the age of forty-one he has done more than most outstanding pastors accomplish in a lifetime. A picture on a church brochure shows him with the serious look of a general. He is the Moses for this church. What is he like?

Dr. Hinkle is a native of Arkansas and was reared in the home of a clergyman. He graduated from Philander Smith College where he earned his bachelor of arts degree. He received further training at Kent College of Law in Chicago and at Northwestern University. He was honored with the doctor of divinity degree by Greenville Industrial College. He is the former pastor of the Greater New Hebron Baptist Church in Little Rock, Arkansas, and the St. Bethel Baptist Church in Chicago Heights, Illinois.

Pastor Hinkle is a strong charismatic figure in the pulpit. He is a handsome man, well dressed, and immaculately groomed. There is a sense of charisma and strength about his personality as he stands behind the sacred desk. When he walks in, the congregation stands, and there is a sense of expectancy that seems to shout, "Our leader has arrived!"

A publication of the church describes an excerpt of the

worship service at the Cathedral of Faith: "On a Sunday morning at the Cathedral, the choir rings out singing, 'Nothing Is Impossible,' and Dr. Hinkle stands quoting Philippians 4:19; Hebrews 11:6; and Acts 17:28. Then he blesses the enthusiastic congregation with love and peace! It radiates throughout the spacious and beautiful cathedral."

As a pulpiteer, Dr. Hinkle is extremely gifted. He has an excellent vocabulary and uses it well to bring out truth from the Word of God in an impressive, articulate manner. He has a knack for alliteration as he speaks. He is a good phrasemaker. He does well at exegeting a passage. He keeps the attention of the audience for an hour as he delivers one of his soul-stirring sermons. He has mastered the art of the old-time Southern Black Baptist preacher who "whoops" his sermon. He is comfortable with the call-and-response pattern in preaching. In fact, the cadence of his preaching is so well timed it is poetry in action. The bittersweet quality of his sound symbolizes the bittersweetness of the black experience—pleasure in the midst of pain.

He knows how to build up to the climax of his message. He moans in between exciting phrases. He "squalls" at the appropriate time at the end of his message with sustained sound. Before he is finished, the audience is standing on its feet testifying to the truth that falls like pearls from the lips of this orator extraordinaire. The style of preaching he uses is reminiscent of the late Rev. C. L. Franklin, Sr. He can "turn out the church." He is no mere emotionalizer. He feeds the flock with the meat of the Word before he gives them the gravy of his cultural tradition. He is one of the best as it relates to the traditional National-Baptist, celebrative worship-experience style. He has "an orchestra in his throat." And he knows how to play the tune of "Thus saith the Lord." He can tell the story movingly and artistically.

One of the obvious characteristics of the Cathedral of

Faith is: there is a demonstrated love and respect for the pastor by the congregation. A publication says, "Dr. Hinkle, loved and respected by his congregation, believes in serving the whole man. He not only teaches his people how to live but also how to make a living." The publication focuses on what folks think about Dr. J. Herbert Hinkle. Dr. Hinkle is a man who has done the following:

1. Implemented an "adopt a senior citizen" program for six years in which young people adopt a senior for the day. Plaques, trophies, and awards are given to outstanding seniors in the community;
2. Transported boys and girls to Sunday School for faith as well as fun;
3. Started the first drug program (Operation Bread Basket) in the city of Inkster and turned it over to the city when it started its own drug program;
4. Knocked on almost every door in the community at least once trying to help the people;
5. Initiated a program to allow all children (black and white) to ride a helicopter for the experience of viewing the city from the air;
6. Provided the first radio to the auxiliary police department of his city;
7. Conducted demonstrations for God and America, repudiating militancy when it was popular;
8. Built and organized a funeral home, day-care center, and Christian day school, in addition to a flower shop to minister to the needs of people;
9. Provided cultural-enrichment experiences for youngsters by transporting them to view the inside of airplanes, zoos, and amusement parks;
10. Traveled on a fact-finding trip to Panama and brought a report back to a bipartisan group;

11. Traveled with senators, congressmen, and laypersons on a goodwill mission to South Africa sponsored by the American government and the South African government;
12. Built a transportation system larger than that of the city of Inkster (once running fifteen buses at one time);
13. Conducted a demonstration against drugs at the state capitol with the approval of the governor;
14. Developed a creative approach to ministering to the needs of the whole person.

Dr. Hinkle is a prolific writer. He has written many articles and provided the text for many publications of the church. He is the author of at least four books including: *These Eternal Truths, Soul-Winning in Black Churches, Handbook for Baptist Churches,* and *How to Reach Multitudes for Christ.*

Dr. Hinkle has led the Cathedral of Faith to be a "major league church." Among the visitors to his church have been such notables as Hank Aaron, Dr. Jack Hyles, Dr. Russell Anderson, Dr. Greg Dickson, Rev. Larry Lawrence, Dr. Martin Luther King, Sr., and Dr. Robert Schuller. In the hallway of the church there is a picture of Dr. Hinkle and the Cathedral choir on the south lawn of the White House in our nation's capital. Jack Hyles said of Dr. Hinkle and the Cathedral of Faith, "This preacher has the vision, and this church has the program." Dr. Robert Schuller said of Dr. Hinkle, "The faith of Dr. Hinkle impresses me."

Growth Through the Sunday School

During its heyday, the Cathedral clearly had the reputation of having the largest Sunday School in the black community. What are some suggestions from the pastor relating to reaching people through the Sunday School? The following are suggestions from the pastor of this church.

Have a solid, Bible-centered message. The Cathedral of Faith is a fundamentalist church. It does not believe in a watered-down view of the Word of God. It bases its message totally upon the Word of God. It has an understanding of the Bible in the classical conservative tradition. It builds its whole message on the foundation of the infallibility of the Scriptures.

Have good methodology. The Cathedral of Faith Sunday School believes that it is possible to have fun and faith together. The methodology employed by this church is often creative and appeals to the excitement instincts of people. For example, on one Sunday, the Sunday School sponsored an "Up, Up, and Away Sunday," in which a helicopter was brought in to provide rides for children as a way of attracting the masses to the Sunday School program.

The pastor must be the leader. The pastor of this church is quite obviously a pro-Sunday-School man. He breathes Sunday School work. He is consumed with reaching people through the Sunday School. He states, "If you expect a people to jump a yard, then you must jump a mile." There is no substitute for the pastor providing leadership in the area of the Sunday School if it is to reach people.

Soul-winning is a must. The Sunday School that would reach people must participate in soul-winning. The church must be built on door-to-door evangelism. There is no substitution for this. The whole church must be involved. The pastor states, "Win the lost at any cost because of Pentecost." In 1975, this church baptized 772 persons. At present it averages baptizing approximately 150 persons per year.

Provide transportation for the participants in Sunday School. This church believes in the bus ministry. In the past it has run as many as fifteen buses and has bused in as many as 500 persons on an average. For special days, they have bused in as many as 1,500. This church has seen great results from a Sunday School bus ministry which has enabled it to exceed the 2,000 attendance mark several times.

Consecrated Sunday School workers are a must. Workers should be led to emphasize the Lordship of Christ in their lives. They should recognize the Holy Spirit as their guide. They should be totally committed to being as Christlike as possible in their life-styles.

Maintain a friendly atmosphere. The Cathedral of Faith has greeters to welcome people to the church. This church believes that a snobbish congregation turns off people and works against effective soul-winning. One is immediately impressed with the friendliness of the people and the pastor at the Cathedral of Faith.

Emphasize tithing. Tithing is taught in the Sunday School as God's way of financing the church. It also enables the church to afford the resources it needs for reaching more people in Sunday School. For example, a tithing church, especially if it has a substantial membership, can mean the difference in whether or not the church has the budget to afford buses for transporting people to the Sunday School.

Promote the Sunday School well. In this church, promotion takes many forms. It starts in the pulpit with the pastor. It extends through the members as they invite persons to Sunday School. It goes off in the form literary publications, through the printing ministry of the church. It is promoted on the air and through any means available to the church.

Make wise use of the media. The Cathedral of Faith utilizes three radio broadcasts (one on WLAC Nashville, Tennessee, extends into twenty-six different states). It has utilized television in the past. And it sends a newsletter to every person in the city of Inkster. It makes use of the media available through modern technology.

Develop a consciousness of largeness. If a church is to reach many people through the Sunday School for the Lord, it must learn to think in terms of many people. This church does not apologize for being large. Rather, it has a rationale for the advantage of the large church. It believes that a large church can meet the needs of the individual better than a small congregation.

Emphasize the priority of the local church. The major emphasis at the Cathedral of Faith is developing the ministry of this local congregation. The pastor does not "run all over town" to every civic meeting. He prioritizes his time for involvement and leadership of the local church.

Have a simple organizational structure. The organizational structure at the Cathedral of Faith is not complex. It is deliberately simple in order to facilitate the implementation of the church program. Dr. Hinkle has said, "So many churches have so many clubs that they club out Jesus." He believes there is power in simplicity.

Provide a good training program for the workers. This church believes in well-trained workers. It believes that people have to pay a price in order to earn the right to work in the Sunday School. Part of the price they must pay is to attend the weekly teachers' meeting. Attendance is mandatory if one wishes to serve as a Sunday School teacher.

The Sunday School program at the Cathedral of Faith is an exciting concept. It has had its day of the mountaintop experience and also its time in the valley. Like the waves of progress, it has continued down through the years under the ministry of a very outstanding and creative pastor. The church is in the process of making "a new beginning." The prevailing feeling is that this Sunday School program which once attracted almost 4,000 persons on one Sunday at Sunday School will be heard from again.

10

The New Shiloh
Saturday Church School
New Shiloh Baptist Church
Baltimore, Maryland
Dr. Harold Carter, Pastor

First Encounter

The spire atop the mammoth Gothic sanctuary points majestically to the sky. The huge structure displays a subtle charm that invites passersby to channel their steps into the monument of intrigue which bears the name: "New Shiloh Baptist Church." The immaculate lawn conspires with the neat overall appearance to transmit body language that proclaims the message, "Here is a great church."

The physical plant at New Shiloh Baptist Church, Baltimore, Maryland, is impressive. It stands as a bridge between an exciting past and a brilliant future. Like an adolescent garment, it has outgrown its maximum effectiveness and anticipates its obsolescence for this congregation as plans have been drawn for an ultramodern new facility.

The sanctuary invites the worshiper into an inner sanctum of spirituality. The atmosphere of reverence reminds the visitor that he is in the presence of God. The multitude of colors, reflected in banners carrying messages about the Divine, emit the impression that this place is alive with the presence of the Lord. A creative mural depicting scenes from the historic black experience surrounds the baptistry and testifies to the relevance of the gospel to the black situation in America. This spacious sanctuary, with its historic cultur-

al motif, reminds the congregation of the partnership between Christianity and social justice. It is a *kerygma* that
preaches the good news that God is a Liberator.

The immediate community of the church is typical of
Baltimore's inner-city dwellings. Characterized by common
walls, miniporches, and concrete yards, this redbrick neighborhood with narrow streets and scarce parking reflects the
anonymity of urbanity which challenges so many churches.
People can be seen sitting on their front steps watching life
pass by. With houses sharing common walls, the neighborhood easily appears to be a collection of urban apartments
insulated by the dynamics of crowded closeness. Yet despite
this insulation and isolation in a sea of people separated by
myriad lifeboat apartments, there seems to be a God-con-
sciousness that permeates the atmosphere.

The general church community served by New Shiloh is
not geographically definable but sociologically identifiable.
The observer readily is impressed with the variety of persons in the membership of this church. The membership
spans the various socioeconomic categories within the black
community. Although the intellectual elite are represented,
one also feels that those with humble academic credentials
feel comfortable. There is an atmosphere of warm acceptance that reaches out to newcomers. In fact, there appears
to be a blend of committed theological scholarship and folksy, pragmatic need meeting in the mind-set of leadership at
New Shiloh. An onlooker may easily be confronted with
evidence that the people attracted to this church prefer
qualitative pastoral leadership with a vision for ministering
to the needs of the community. People from all social strata
have this preference, and they are found involved in the
ministry of this church.

Church Roots

New Shiloh Baptist Church is a pioneer of creativity in religious education in the black community. How did this church become a pacesetter whose model is emulated across the country? What is the story of its history? In his book *Determined: A Faith History of a People Determined to Live with Christ,* Dr. Harold A. Carter focuses attention on two relevant questions about the story of New Shiloh: "How could it be that this congregation, located in the heart of one of America's urban cities, Baltimore, Maryland, would survive, prosper, and continue to grow? How could it be that this congregation of 3,500 persons would band together as one and move forward from generation to generation as a church determined to live with Christ?"[1]

The New Shiloh story goes back to the beginning of the twentieth century, when there was a black migration from the South to the urban North. Thousands of blacks migrated to Baltimore, Maryland, in search of a better quality of life than offered by the system in the South.

These transplanted Southerners brought the religion of their culture with them. One of the practices endemic to the new migrants was the community prayer band. According to Carter, "Through prayer bands, Black people kept alive traditional folk songs, called on God without artificial restrictions, and quite often laid the foundation for churches to follow."[2] Perhaps inadvertently, the black prayer band movement led to the expression of a distinct form of black church planting.

New Shiloh Baptist Church was one of the churches that grew out of the prayer-band movement. In October, 1902, Rev. Whit W. Allen organized and founded this church on a base that began with three persons in a prayer band. The first name selected was the Shiloh Free Baptist Church. In

1907 the name was changed to Shiloh Baptist Church, and in 1926 the word *New* was added to the name. During the ministry of "Dr. Allen," as he was affectionately known, the church experienced phenomenal growth, and its membership totaled some five thousand persons.

Allen served as pastor of this church for forty years and earned the designation of having been "loyal to the pew." His long, fruitful ministry endeared him to the hearts of his parishioners. He is remembered as "a powerful preacher," a firm believer in the absolute truth of the Bible, and a fatherly figure with a winsome personality with which people could identify. This charismatic leader led his church to win people to Christ with evangelistic zeal. He built a massive church with a broad appeal involved in ministering to the community. This deeply respected, loved, venerated, and emulated pulpiteer laid a strong foundation upon which the church would continue to build in the future.

On Palm Sunday, 1942, the Lord called Dr. Allen to his eternal reward. The mantle of leadership fell on Dr. J. Timothy Boddie, a pastor with theological training at Virginia Seminary and College, Lynchburg, Virginia. Dr. Boddie assumed the pastorate of New Shiloh in 1942. An assessment of the Boddie leadership has been stated thus:

> This ministerial team was able to lead the church from a gathering of persons, loosely held together into a church of strong, biblical, purposeful discipleship where members began to understand and support some of the deeper demands of the faith.[3]

During the Boddie administration huge progress was made. Under the leadership of the pastor's wife, the talented Emory Boddie, missions emphases were given priority, and involvement of women in missions increased. A program of

biblical stewardship was instituted which yielded systematically greater income for church programs. During this
period the involvement of the church expanded into
denominational and ecumenical circles. Dr. Boddie's
twenty-one-year pastorate ended in 1963.

In 1964 New Shiloh called the twenty-eight-year-old
Harold A. Carter to be pastor. The coming of the young
pastor and his lovely wife, Weptanoma, brought a new
sense of excitement to the church. The civil rights movement was at its zenith. Dr. Martin Luther King, Jr., was the
unquestioned moral leader of the day in the estimation of
the black community. The church had been cast into a prophetic leadership role for the cause of black liberation. Black
churches had caught a vision of possibilities with young
pastoral leadership. Harold Carter seemed to embody the
best in the relevant black pastoral tradition.

In Harold A. Carter, New Shiloh had called one of God's
strong servants to be the spiritual leader. He had already
graduated from Alabama State University and earned a
divinity degree with honors from Crozier Theological Seminary. Yet his brilliant mind still sought more academic challenges. He had pastored the Court Street Baptist Church in
Lynchburg, Virginia, one of America's oldest black Baptist
churches. He was an associate of Dr. Martin Luther King's
and had been involved in "the movement." He was blessed
with a talented wife whose gifts would enable her to have
an impact in her own right. Blessed with a brilliant, analytical mind, Harold Carter would soon escalate the involvement of the congregation into new creative approaches to
ministry, especially in the area of Sunday School.

New Shiloh Baptist Church has a rich history. Its roots go
back to the turn of the century. It has experienced remark-
able growth in members. It has been led by only three pastors in its eighty-three-year history. It has not been afraid

of change. Perhaps a dominant view of the church may be seen through Carter's statement:

> While the church has had its growing problems, it has always managed to maintain a great love for the proclaimed Word, a contagious sense of celebration, and a fierce love and loyalty to Jesus Christ.[4]

The Shepherd

Upon meeting pastor Harold A. Carter, one quickly becomes impressed with his spirituality. He seems to be a shepherd who walks close to the Lord. His conversation reveals the heart of a man deeply dedicated to God and committed to letting God do great things through his ministry at and beyond New Shiloh Baptist Church.

Carter was born in Selma, Alabama, and was reared the son of a minister. His proximity to a "man of the cloth" left him with the desire to strive for the best level of theological education. After graduating with honors from Crozier Theological Seminary in Chester, Pennsylvania, he pursued the rigorous task of taking two earned doctorates simultaneously. In May 1976, he had the distinction of earning the doctor of ministry degree from Colgate-Rochester Divinity School *and* the doctor of philosophy degree in theology magna cum laude from Saint Mary's Seminary.

Dr. Carter is in worldwide demand as a major speaker for evangelistic events. His preaching opportunities have taken him to some twenty-five different countries. Many places in Europe, Africa, the Philippines, Romania, and the Carribbean have been exposed to his messages. Major denominations in the United States such as Southern Baptists, American Baptists, Progressive Baptists, Methodists, and Assemblies of God use him frequently. He was one of the keynote speakers in 1981 at the American Festival of Evangelism in Kansas City, Missouri, at which 15,000 persons participated in an event to "call America to Christ."

Dr. Carter is a gifted pulpiteer. He is blessed with an appealing "preacher's voice" that allows its baritone message to be delivered with force. His voice has been described as sounding similar to that of the late Dr. Martin Luther King. This medium-sized prophet has been bequeathed a mighty voice that enables him to drill his point home convincingly. The content of his message is heavy but simple. "Carter seeks to grab the most unsophisticated minds in his congregation."[5] He says, "If I can reach the lowest common denominator, I believe I will have preached the authentic gospel. What's going through my mind is how do you make tangible the weighty truth of the Scripture so that the simplest minds can grasp it?"[6] To put it differently, he has the gift of discovering deep truths of God's Word and sharing the profound simply. Although he is unquestionably a gifted academician, his messages are not pedantic or stilted. He uses his brilliance to simplify the great mysteries of life.

As a preacher, Carter has managed to blend two powerful forces in the pulpit—intellectual ability and oratorical skill. Nobody will ever accuse him of being "an egg head," and nobody will say, "He can't preach." The evidence is too overwhelming in the other direction.

His pulpit skills have been widely recognized. Not only is he a word craftsman, but he has something to say forcefully. His messages have ministered to the thousands fed from their wisdom and spiritual power. His messages are interpretations of Scripture which bring hope to the individual with a heavy use of the anecdote wrapped in the sermonic style of the Southern black preacher. One of New Shiloh's members who has heard numerous sermons by Carter described the experience like this: "Creative counseling masses of people but also seemingly speaking with the thought of one person in mind. He preaches so as to bring the future hopes of a people into present reality. His knack of using ever-recurring anecdotes to drive home truths keeps his messages fresh and alive."[7]

Dr. Harold Carter not only is a giant in the pulpit, he is as able with the pen as he is with the Sword of the Spirit. Not only is he a great orator, he is also a great journalist. This prolific writer has authored several books including *The Prayer Tradition of Black People, Myths That Mire the Ministry, The Preaching of Jonah, Determined: A Faith History of a People Determined to Live with Christ,* and others in process. He has also contributed to numerous magazines and scholarly publications.

One cannot help but be impressed with the skills of the pastor in the area of teaching. The full weight of his theological training enriches the class taught by the pastor on Saturday mornings. Hundreds of adults flock to be fed by the shepherd each week in the Saturday church school class he teaches. Enthusiastic minds eagerly sit at the feet of this master teacher to soak up pearls of wisdom. One senses a reverence from the class for the great mind but humble spirit of the pastor. One senses that the audience does not hesitate to ask difficult questions because their teacher probably knows the answer. Sitting in Dr. Carter's class is like taking an expedition into the deep truths of God's Word. He brings out information rarely addressed in a class.

In summary, New Shiloh has been blessed by the continued tradition of being led by an outstanding pastor—in the person of Dr. Harold A. Carter. This scholar, educator, pulpiteer, and leader has a vision of where the Lord wants his church to go.

The Flock

New Shiloh Baptist Church is located in the heart of urban Baltimore. The congregation is composed of about 3,500 active members. It has a rich history and looks forward to a glorious future. Blessed with outstanding pastoral leadership, it is famous for its ongoing ministries of missions and evangelism. For more than a decade it has maintained multistaffed ministries with a minister at large, minister of music, and minister of education. During the tenure of Dr. Carter more than 40 persons have surrendered to the ministry. At least fifteen persons now serve as ministers who were ordained by New Shiloh under the Carter pastorate. With an annual budget of about $800,000, the church baptizes about 325 persons a year!

This church has an holistic approach to ministry, being concerned about the total person. It practices both fervent evangelism and aggressive social concern. Some of the ministries of the church include:

A radio ministry on at least three stations, including a broadcast in Haiti;

A food co-op ministry with deliveries every other week through the New Shiloh Food Co-op;

A ministry of printed literature including books by Pastor and Mrs. Carter;

A scholarship assistance ministry for high school graduates;

A seminarian financial assistance ministry for students pursuing theological training;

A prison ministry at penal institutions;

A visitation ministry at boys' homes;

A financial-support ministry for colleges, seminaries, and numerous social concerns;

A Saturday church school ministry which provides Bible, academic, worship, and spiritually artistic growth. This program has been a model for numerous churches across the nation.

Other traditional ministries are also carried on by the church.

The guiding principles of New Shiloh are reflected in a statement by the pastor which reveals the heartbeat of this great church:

New Shiloh therefore declares publicly to absolute belief in the Bible, God's Holy Word, the inherent sinfulness of all humanity, and the consequent necessity to preach the Gospel, calling men from a life of sin to fullness in the kingdom of God. New Shiloh believes in the Mystical Body of Christ, the fellowship of Saints, and the fact that born-again believers can live in peaceable love and holy fellowship. To this end, this church seeks to be a saving station, celebrating God and meeting human needs in the day and time God has called to serve. All officers and elected officials are called upon to publicly declare their faith and allegiance to Christ and His Word, year after year. This public service of reaffirmation and rededication is a source of renewed honesty and sincerity to the sacred cause of our Lord.[8]

The secret to the success of New Shiloh Baptist Church seems to be the powerful combination of a super pastor with a vision, a congregation with the commitment to follow God's leadership, and a determination to live for Christ on the part of both pastor and people.

The Alternative to Sunday School

One of the interesting programs at New Shiloh is the Saturday Church School. Whereas most churches have a *Sunday* School, New Shiloh has a *Saturday* church school! How did this alternative to Sunday School develop? Why did the church move Sunday School to Saturday? The story goes back to 1972. That year the pastor became burdened about the existence of a mini Sunday School at New Shiloh. The church was most ineffective in reaching many of its members for Sunday School. Dr. Carter concluded, "But twelve years ago, as this urban congregation of three thousand members and fewer than 200 in Sunday School looked at its Christian education program, it had to admit that real attention needed to be given to this fundamental need."[9] In response to this conclusion, an exploratory committee was formed to develop specific recommendations for the improvement of the quality of the Sunday School.

The exploratory committee recommended that the church move its Sunday School program to Saturday beginning in October 1973. The overhaul of the religious education program at New Shiloh yielded other recommendations including:

(1) Become more Bible centered and supplement with reference books and Christian literature we would write ourselves.

(2) Discontinue Sunday School as an organized department and put all energies into Saturday church school development.

(3) Departmentalize the Saturday church school providing elective classes for academic enrichment, arts, and crafts.

(4) Go into the community and publicize widely making Saturday church school an outreach ministry.

(5) Follow the Christian year in worship emphasis, dramas, programs, and celebrations.

(6) Consciously seek to be evangelistic in Christian teachings and family oriented towards building a new respect for parental authority, guidance, and the Christian pursuit of love.[10]

The church accepted these recommendations and moved to implement this mammoth challenge. The new Saturday church school idea was promoted and publicized through posters, radio announcements, word-of-mouth communication, and from the pulpit. On the first Saturday in October 1973, the Saturday church school became a reality at New Shiloh. Not only had a new concept in religious education been implemented, but some one thousand persons enrolled! With a change of meeting day and curriculum, the church school enrollment had increased 400 percent!

The implementation of the Saturday church school program had a tremendous impact on the congregation at New Shiloh. The huge success of this new approach brought several dividends to the church. The church was different in these ways:

First, an unexpected dividend was "a swelling tide of evangelism." The Saturday Church School became a catalyst for soul-winning. The pastor reported, "Parents who sent their children to the Saturday school began coming to the church and were won to the cause of Christ."[11] After the Saturday church school started, baptisms at the church jumped from sixteen per month to an average of thirty-five per month.

A second benefit of the new arrangement was an increase in worship service attendance on Sunday. Greater involvement in Saturday church school generated more involvement in Sunday worship. New Shiloh had to add another

Sunday worship service to accommodate the crowds stimu-
lated by the Saturday experience.

A surprising phenomenon developed into a third dividend: professionals in the congregation, notably public
school and college teachers, "rose to the challenge" and
became willing to sacrifice for "the movement." Yet it was
extremely difficult to enlist their participation in the local
church, and especially in Sunday School. The Saturday
church school created a challenge to academically trained
minds to dedicate their talents to the Lord. These professionals enthusiastically became involved in the "renaissance
of Christian education" at New Shiloh.

A fourth benefit to the church was an increase in fellowship between faculty and students. The sacrifices of Saturday for a weekly religious-education event has not proved
to be a problem. Instead of shying away from attendance,
teachers and pupils can often be found talking and fellowshipping after official adjournment. The traditional Sunday
School schedule had not made this fellowshipping time
practical.

A fifth point of impact was in the area of modifying the
schedule. The Saturday church school schedule was set up
as follows:

10:00 AM   General Worship
10:30 AM   Bible Study (all classes)
11:30 AM   Second Period Classes
           Bible
           Recording/writing/arts
           crafts/typing/cooking
           carpentry/computers/etc.
12:30 PM   Assembly - A closing devotion from each
           class
 1:00 PM   Adjourn

During July, August, and part of September the schedule is reduced to two hours, from 10:00 AM to noon. The regular term runs from September through June. This combination provides opportunity for renewal, rest, and rejuvenation in preparation for an enthusiastic fall kickoff.

Dividend number six is the design and implementation of nontraditional curriculum. Whereas traditional Sunday Schools usually restrict curricula to various Bible study emphases, New Shiloh, however, has broadened class offerings. In the Saturday church school a participant can study courses ranging from Genesis to creative dance. Their curriculum focuses on training people to meet life's needs. It is practically oriented. It is more than an attempt to teach people the Word, it is an effort to supply the specifics of implementing the implications of the Word where people live.

A seventh characteristic reflected through the Saturday church school was a dramatic jump in enrollment and average attendance. Enrollment increased from below 200 to about 1,000; average attendance ranged between 400 to 600. One sure conclusion about the new approach is that it was effective in securing the involvement of many more people. The church creatively attempted to meet the needs of people, and the effort was met with a tremendous response.

The enrollment of adults was another surprising development as a result of the Saturday church school program. In most Sunday Schools in the black community, the "children's syndrome" is operative. In this syndrome, adults are not expected to participate in Sunday School because "Sunday School is for children only." However, adult attendance jumped dramatically. On a typical Saturday, half the people present are adults involved in creative classes. For many adults the Saturday church school is the first formal learning experience within the context of care and concern.

Perhaps one of the most significant outgrowths of this creative approach was the ministry. Seventeen persons who came through New Shiloh's Saturday church school now pastor churches!

Once New Shiloh ventured into a creative alternative to its sparsely attended Sunday School program, exciting surprises were discovered. As a result of the Saturday church school, this servant church in the heart of Baltimore would never be the same.

A major distinctive of New Shiloh's program is the creative curriculum. The church embraced the philosophy of expanding a traditional Sunday School curriculum. While their curriculum starts with basic Bible study, additional courses complement the biblical foundations. For example, courses are offered in recording, creative writing, arts, crafts, typing, cooking, carpentry, computer operation, and other areas. They have recovered the generalist curriculum emphases of the black Sunday School movement of a century ago.

Several other ministries have grown out of the Saturday church school at New Shiloh. These spin-offs include:

(1) A tutorial program three days a week in which assistance is available in English, Latin, Spanish, French, math, reading, and typing;

(2) A "Youth Express" class in which current problems affecting teenagers are discussed from a Christian perspective;

(3) A class for the hearing impaired;

(4) The sponsoring of "festival days" by the church "where teachers set up booths, sometimes blocking off the street in front of the church for an old-time country fair usually built around a family theme;"[12]

(5) Marches involving 2,000 people "celebrating family solidarity in Christ;"
(6) A weekly witnessing ministry in a home of delinquent boys.

What is the key to success for New Shiloh's Saturday church school? From the perspective of the church, three major factors may be mentioned.

The most evident dynamic that makes New Shiloh's Saturday church school successful is the leadership role of the pastor. The vision and charisma of Dr. Harold Carter permeate this ministry. Without his leadership and involvement, it probably would not thrive as it does. He says, "A further key is the total involvement of the pastor. I have taught a weekly Adult Bible class, sharing truths about various books of Scripture and concerns in Christian theology. This class of 100 has proved to be a nucleus of inner strength and power around which the rest of the program could build."[13] The New Shiloh testimony is that the most important ingredient in a church school program is the leadership of the pastor.

Another dynamic contribution to the success of the Saturday church school is an effective leadership-development program. Prior to serving as a teacher in the church school, prospective workers are required to complete a leadership development program. In the leadership development program, future teachers are taught how to "be genuinely Christian, evangelical in their beliefs, and committed to the practice of soul-winning and serving others."[14] Furthermore, attendance at weekly teachers' meetings enables the faculty to discuss class-related problems, receive training in outreach, develop skills in retaining new members, and preview the upcoming lesson. Clearly, a strength of the church school is trained leadership.

The opening worship service also provides a dynamic impact for the Saturday experience. Built with creativity in mind, the worship period involves guest choirs, musical groups, bands, and notable personalities. The worship period not only sets the mood for the educational experience but provides another opportunity for various components of the worship service to be exercised. The New Shiloh model assumes that proper learning occurs in the context of worship.

Would New Shiloh go back to the traditional Sunday School? The pastor responds with an emphatic "No! We have a catchall class for those who come to our church at 9:30 on Sunday morning, not knowing about our Saturday program. But our dedication is to the ongoing enrichment of the Saturday Church School."[15] This church has tried an alternative to Sunday School, and they like it.

An Analysis of Success

From the standpoint of Sunday School growth strategy, what appears to be the formula for effectiveness for this super church? What are some characteristics that make the Saturday church school effective at New Shiloh? The following seem to be components of New Shiloh's strategy:

1. *A pastor with the vision.*—The observer immediately becomes aware that the pastor of New Shiloh has a broad vision for reaching people through relevant religious education. An interview with Dr. Carter reveals a heartfelt burden for helping people achieve their potential. He sees the potential for people-building that rests in the resources of a congregation that dares to be relevant. He understands the opportunity for improving the quality of life for congregants who move beyond the usual worship experience to involvement in a first-rate training program. This shepherd has a

grasp of the difference a church can make in the life of the community if it is willing to pay the price. This pastor knows: "Where there is no vision the people perish."[16]

2. *The personal involvement of the pastor.*—At New Shiloh the guiding force behind the Saturday church school is the pastor. He does not abdicate his leadership role. He leads; he does not point. He has credibility because he role models involvement; he avoids the subterfuge of token participation; he is physically present and significantly involved in the Saturday church school. This program is important to the life of the church because the pastor, the official legitimizer for the congregation, makes it his personal priority.

3. *A distinctive definition.*—The definition of the church school at New Shiloh is distinctive. It is not simply "the Bible-teaching arm of the church." It is broader. It involves the church preparing people for thorough ministry. Therefore, this church school program extends beyond the traditional definition. It does not simply help people understand the content of the Bible; it helps people prepare for life situations.

4. *A creative curriculum.*—The curriculum at New Shiloh's Saturday Church School is creative. Geared to meet the needs of people, it dares to corral available resources to equip people for life. Practical courses such as carpentry, typing, and computer training entrance many people who would not likely be interested in the traditional Sunday School curriculum. The success of the creative approach to the Saturday church school at New Shiloh shows that people tend to respond when their needs are met.

5. *A preferred schedule.*—The scheduled time for the church school is apparently preferred by the New Shiloh congregation. The meeting time—Saturday mornings—is obviously better for this church. Perhaps some of the dynamics of the traditional meeting time for Sunday School worked against

encouraging people to attend. Not only does the new schedule provide a different meeting day, but it allows for more time spent in church school. Consequently, the participants can benefit from exposure to more training by virtue of spending more time in class per week. The response of the congregation indicates a preference for the new schedule.

6. *An emphasis on adults.*—Adults make up half of the average attendance at the church school at New Shiloh. The church has not written off the adults; they have challenged them. As a result, they are involved. At this congregation, church school is not for children only; it is for the family. They have discovered that if we reach the adults, the children will be brought also.

7. *A commitment to growth.*—This church was ready to make a definite commitment to grow through the church school. Growing out of a burden of the pastor to reach more people, the congregation embraced the concept that it needed to be willing to pay the price for growing. They realized that a fundamental component of growth strategy is making the commitment to grow. Commitment supplied the energy that propelled this new approach to church school.

8. *Proper worker enlistment and training.*—The selection and training of workers at New Shiloh's church school is a sacred task. Painstaking care is taken to enlist committed and dedicated teachers for the church school. In-depth qualitative training is provided. There is an atmosphere filled with the attitude that "we want to do our best." The weekly teachers' meeting provides opportunity for training to be effective.

9. *The provision of space and equipment.*—A major concern at New Shiloh is the provision of space and equipment. The church knows that space and equipment are major factors in the effective educational experience. Their new church building has a provision for even more educational space. This church understands the relationship between a max-

imum learning environment and the providing of adequate space and equipment.

10. *A Bible-centered evangelism.*—Although there are many courses in New Shiloh's creative curriculum, the basic foundation is built upon an appreciation for the Word of the Lord. The Bible is the basic textbook in this church school. It is taught with a twofold emphasis: (1) winning people to Christ and (2) equipping them for service. Evangelism is the major thrust of this Bible-centered church school.

The above characteristics provide some insights into the success of the Saturday church school at New Shiloh Baptist Church. This creative alternative to the traditional Sunday School yielded with the combining of the classical Sunday School curriculum with a practical program of Christian social ministries. For this dually aligned Progressive Baptist and American Baptist church, an experiment with boldness and creativity paid off.

NOTES

1. Harold A. Carter, *Determined: A Faith History of a People Determined to Live with Christ!* (Baltimore, MD: Gateway Press, Inc., 1984), p. 1.

2. Ibid., p. 3.

3. Ibid., p. 7.

4. Ibid., p. 9.

5. Ibid., p. 19.

6. Ibid.

7. Ibid.

8. Ibid., p. 101.

9. Ibid., p. 22.

10. Ibid., p. 23.

11. Quoted in *Leadership 100,* Jan.-Feb., 1983, p. 15.

12. Carter, Ibid., p. 17.

13. Ibid.

14. Ibid.

15. Ibid.

16. Ibid.

11

Sunday School Growth in the Black Community

Our study of ten super Sunday Schools in the black community has yielded considerable information as it relates to the question of Sunday School growth in the black community. This investigation has revealed many insights related to reaching the black community through the Sunday School. Of this we are certain, based on this inquiry: It is possible under the proper conditions to reach large numbers of black persons for the Sunday School.

There appears to be a proper combination of dynamics that make it possible to have an effective Sunday School program in a church. The church community in American today is deeply indepted to these churches that serve as powerful prototypic models but prove that it is possible to experience tremendous Sunday School growth.

How do these churches manage to build a super Sunday School? What commonalities are present in their approaches? Some general observations are in order relating to analyzing the dynamics of these super Sunday Schools in the black community.

General Observations

1. *The pastor's readiness is the crucial issue that makes the difference in whether the Sunday School will experience tremendous growth.* A

unifying characteristic woven through experience of all these Sunday Schools proves the fact that the pastor is the key. Unless the pastor has a vision for the Sunday School, then it will not be an effective Sunday School. This is not a program of the church that can be left entirely up to laypersons. The pastor must lead out. He must be ready.

This observation yields the following questions for the pastor. Does he have the philosophy that growth through the Sunday School ought to be a top priority in his ministry? Is he committed to building the church through the Sunday School? Is he aware of the vast resources and programs available to assist a Sunday School in its effort to grow? Is he involved in the Sunday School? The experience of our churches in the study group reveals that unless the pastor is ready to lead, the church will not be ready to grow through the Sunday School.

2. *The type of Sunday School program makes a difference.* A church usually has an effective Sunday School growth-wise only if it uses a growth-oriented Sunday School program. There are basically two types of Sunday School programs: the growth-oriented Sunday School program and the teaching-oriented Sunday School program. The growth-oriented Sunday School programs prioritize growth, understand basics of Sunday School growth, and implant growth principles to reach people through Sunday School, in addition to providing excellent Bible-teaching experiences. It should be noted that most of these churches in our study with super Sunday Schools are Southern Baptist churches in the black community and use the Southern Baptist Sunday School program. It may be argued that even the others which are not Southern Baptist churches also use the principles found in the Southern Baptist Sunday School program. The point is that the Southern Baptist Sunday School program is a growth-oriented program and embodies those proven principles of

growth that are so effective in the black community. It is estimated that at least twelve other denominations use the Southern Baptist Sunday School program in principle. All of the Sunday School programs experiencing tremendous growth today are using these growth principles.

A major implication from the observation that the type of Sunday School program used makes a difference is this: Pastors should be aware of the qualitative differences in various Sunday School programs and select the approaches that are built on tried and proven success principles. The greatest question that can be asked and should be asked about a potential Sunday School approach under consideration by a pastor is: "Does it work?"

3. *Commitment to growth through the Sunday School is a priority.* While there are many ways to grow a church, these churches have in common the commitment to grow through the Sunday School. A good question for discussion is whether it makes any difference about the way a church grows. Some churches emphasize having an electrifying music program as a strategy for growth. Others emphasize dynamic preaching and soul-stirring worship experiences. Others emphasize social concern and social-action involvement. Even others focus on building the family unit as a strategy. Does it really make a difference the way a church chooses to grow? As it relates to these churches, it does apparently make a difference. It makes so much of a difference that they choose to make their priority growing through the Sunday School.

What this means to the church is summed up in these principles.

1. *It means that a pastor must have the philosophy that the Sunday School is the most effective way to grow a church.*

2. *It may mean that a pastor may wish to combine two or more strong emphases areas, including the Sunday School, as a high priority for growing the church.*

3. *It may mean that the church will have to be sold or converted to the point of view that Sunday School growth can be a very effective way of church growth.*

4. *Potential members are systematically identified and enlisted.* These churches with super Sunday Schools know who their prospects are. They have a prospect file; there is a list with the names of persons who could be coming to their Sunday School program if properly and persistently invited. They do not go after "everybody" with a scatter-gun approach. They go after specific individuals who have been identified as prospects for involvement in their Sunday School program.

This means that every church wishing to grow through the Sunday School needs to have an excellent up-to-date prospect file. Sunday School growth methodology recommends that a church have a prospect file with at least the number of prospects equal to the number of persons it has enrolled. A church may have to start a prospect file.

5. *There is a willingness to start new teaching units.* These churches are not hesitant in starting new classes. They realize that one of the trends in Sunday School growth is that new classes tend to grow faster than older classes. Therefore, a class should be started when a church wants to reach people. It should not be started only when the old class is bursting at the seams. This philosophy is part of a growth approach to reach more people through the Sunday School.

What this means for a church is that workers and members need to be oriented to the point of view that they can multiply by dividing. Class size should be generally consistent with the guidelines for ideal class size based on the best of Sunday School science.

6. *The selection of workers is made with the greatest care.* One of the common points of all of these Sunday Schools is that they have good, strong workers. Great care is taken in the selection of those who work in Sunday School. For these church-

es, worker selection is a sacred task. Standards and qualifications should be taken into consideration when workers are selected. Deep seasons of prayer should proceed the selection of those who work in the Sunday School.

An implication for careful worker selection means that churches will need to set and enforce standards for those who would work in Sunday School. There is no room in a growth-oriented Sunday School for the slothful worker or the uncommitted person who just routinely accepts the job of working in Sunday School for another year. Ideally, the persons who are selected as Sunday School workers ought to be those who feel that God has called them to serve.

7. *The churches make sure that all of the workers receive first-rate training.* The conclusion of these pastors is that trained workers make all the difference in the world. They see their churches as having a responsibility to make sure that when persons commit themselves to work in Sunday School, they will receive the best available training to equip them to do so effectively and efficiently.

Churches that accept this challenge must then have qualitative training programs for their Sunday School workers. Sometimes these are provided through denominational sources. Other times, the churches may have to create them.

8. *Sufficient teaching space is made available.* In the churches with the super Sunday Schools, there is a great effort made in providing adequate teaching space for Sunday School. Space is wisely utilized in the educational facility. Some churches have well-developed Sunday School classrooms in very efficient educational buildings. For example, the largest Sunday School in our study was also the one that had the largest amount of Sunday School classrooms.

What this means for the church is that more attention needs to be given to providing adequate teaching space for the Sunday School if it expects to experience Sunday School growth. Inadequate space can actually work against the growing of a Sunday School.

9. *Workers are expected to attend a meaningful Weekly Workers' Meeting.* In our churches with the super Sunday Schools, the Weekly Workers' Meeting is a very important part of the Sunday School growth process. It is not merely a casual appendage. It is an integral part of being ready to produce a growth-oriented Sunday School.

Resources are available that will show churches how to have a dynamic, productive Weekly Workers' Meeting. This should be a time of the greatest importance in preparing to grow a dynamic Sunday School.

10. *The Sunday School has an effective visitation program.* The growing Sunday School usually has a Weekly Visitation Program. It does not sit back and wait for people to decide on their own that they want to come to their Sunday School. The church is militantly involved in going after people.

11. *In-depth Bible study is the foundation of the curriculum.* The Bible is the textbook in our super Sunday Schools. Even when the curriculum is broadened to include other emphases, the Bible is still the primary textbook. In-depth Bible study feeds the deepest needs of persons and motivates them to return to the Sunday School for this worthwhile experience.

What this means for churches is that they should provide more than a superficial experience in studying the Bible. They should major on providing answers to all of the questions of life relating to the Word of God.

12. *There is an emphasis on involving adults in the Sunday School.* Our super Sunday Schools have an unusually high number of adults attending. They have apparently rejected the idea that if you get the child you will get the parent. For them it works the other way: when you get the parent you will get the child.

Churches have an immense challenge in reaching adults through the Sunday School. Strategies should be devised for enlisting adult participation and involvement.

13. *The Sunday School class should provide an opportunity to minister to the total needs of persons.* In the Sunday School approach of the churches in our study there is an emphasis on the ministry dimension. A Sunday School class is more than just a Bible-teaching session. It is a small-group context where people care about each other and help meet each other's needs.

Churches need to explore the possibilities of involving their members in ministry to one another through the Sunday School methodology. This can be an effective network for doing the work of the ministry in the church.

14. *Personal evangelism permeates the Sunday School program.* In our churches with super Sunday Schools, evangelism is a priority. They have a vision for the lost and a commitment to introduce people to a saving knowledge of the Lord Jesus Christ. The Sunday School classroom is a place where evangelism is implemented. The Sunday School teacher and worker are expected to be effective soul-winners. Workers in the Sunday School are expected to be involved with their members and prospects to make sure that they have an opportunity to have a right relationship with God.

For the church this means that evangelistic training is a must for Sunday School workers. Reports have indicated that of all of the persons in the United States who are not enrolled in an evangelistic-type Sunday School, the chances are only 1 in 264 that they will ever accept Christ and be baptized. However, of those persons who are involved in an evangelistic-type Sunday School, the chances are 1 in 3 that they will find Jesus as Lord and Savior. What an effective way to reach people for Christ!